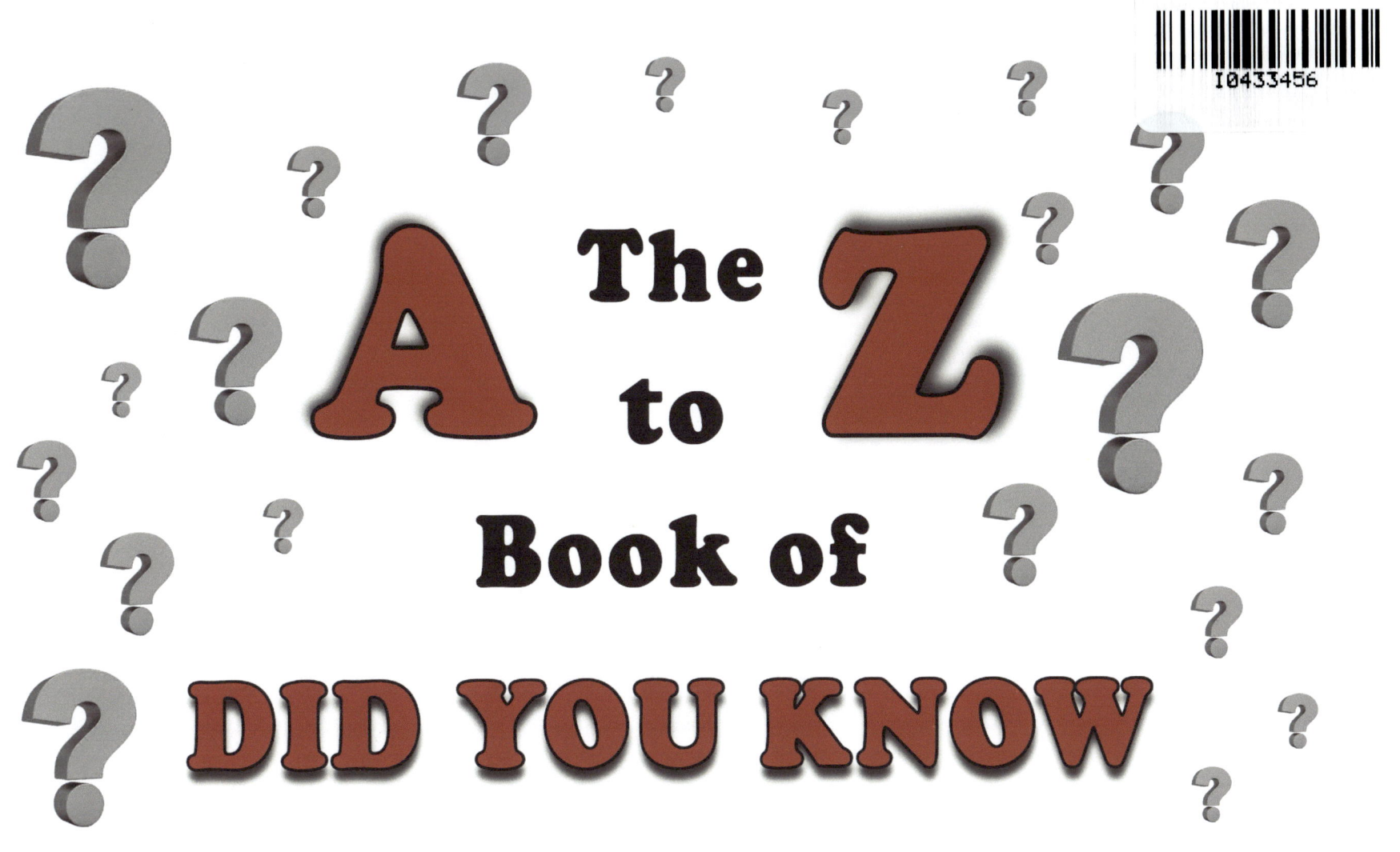

The A to Z Book of DID YOU KNOW

Guaranteed: Something you didn't know

Michael P. Earney

© Copyright Michael P. Earney 2019 All Rights reserved.

No part of this book may be reproduced, stored in a retrieval system, or transmitted by any means, electronic, mechanical, photocopying, recording, or otherwise, without written permission from the author.

ISBN-13: 978-1-941345-67-2 PB

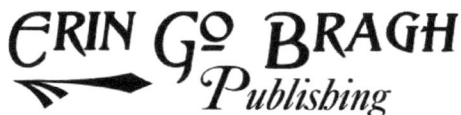

Canyon Lake, TX

www.ErinGoBraghPublishing.com

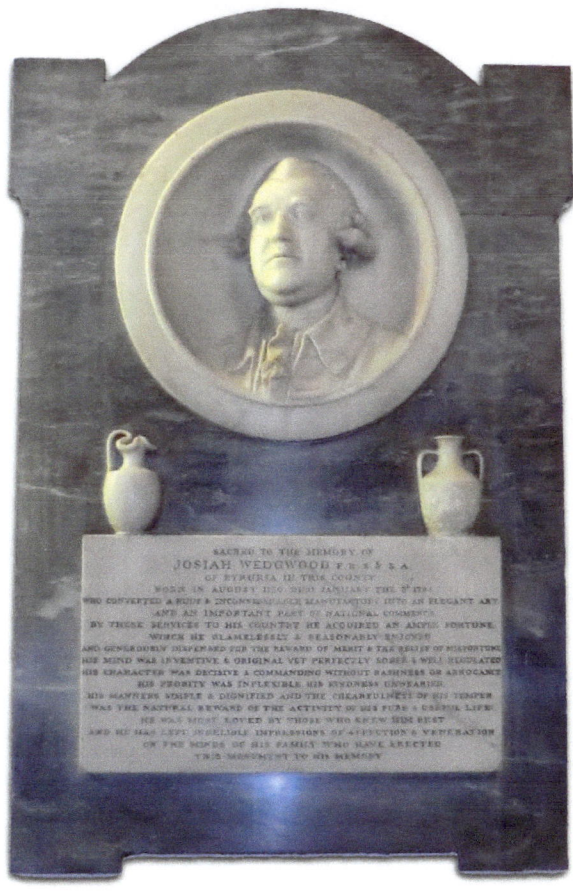

Did you know that **Josiah Wedgewood**, who is credited with the industrialization of pottery production, was a pioneer of the "satisfaction or your money back guarantee"? Using this guarantee, he shipped unsolicited pottery to potential clients across Europe. Most businesses today follow the same strategy, knowing, just as Wedgewood did, that it will attract customers even though most will never take advantage of the guarantee due either to the loss of a receipt, laziness, procrastination, because of the guarantee time limit or any number of other reasons. Josiah Wedgewood was also a prominent slavery abolitionist and the grandfather of Charles Darwin.

Humbly dedicated to Mr. Smarty Pants, who has entertained and informed me and countless others over the years.

"There are more things in heaven and earth, Horacio, than are dreamt of in your philosophy."

— Hamlet (Act 1, Scene 5) William Shakespeare (1564-1616)

Did you know the first folio (1623) reads "*our* philosophy?" Since Hamlet and Horacio went to the same university it would be normal to assume they shared the same philosophy but in this scene Horacio is having trouble believing that the ghost of Hamlet's father is speaking to him. The later version suggests they no longer share a common belief system.

"The A to Z book of Did You Know"

This addition to the A to Z series delves into the realms of general and esoteric knowledge, things we should know, things we thought we knew and things you never before thought about. It's a fun, eclectic collection that is guaranteed to provide many 'Gee whiz!' moments and interesting information with which you can stun friends and family alike. Fittingly, the illustrations also come from a wide range of sources and will surprise and delight you. There is no doubt that owning this book will add to your knowledge, improve your diet and increase brain cells. Or your money back!

If I knew

If I knew all there was to know

would I be wise, would I have more dough?

Or would confusion rule my days

as I chose between the yea's and nay's

of what is right and what is wrong

make sage decisions all day long.

If I were judge of every case

the losing side I'd have to face.

My every word I'd have to weigh

that this must go but this can stay

Contentious views would fill the air

can being right as well be fair?

When certitude gives way to doubt

it may be wisest to step out

Or wiser yet, let it be said,

just empty out my aching head.

Michael P. Earney 2019

Did you know there are many things that nobody knows?

Knowledge is often nothing more than an interpretation of observed phenomena, as variable as the minds through which it passes. Certain things that are known can prove to be mistaken in the light of further knowledge. When this happens, the earlier knowledge becomes merely a belief. Very often the belief is preferred to the new knowledge. Experts and those we look to for guidance are very often the biggest offenders when it comes to being sources of knowledge. What we learn and then know is not knowledge in the wider sense, but what is known, unknown, believed and disbelieved is in constant flux as new ideas, new understandings, new observations and sometimes, lost knowledge rediscovered, expands our body of knowledge. The amount of knowledge available to us is, at this point in time, greater than at any other time in the past. Yet the persistence of willful ignorance, the insistence on clinging to ideas, beliefs and so called 'truths' that have long been discarded as invalid, remains. If we know anything, it is that everything is an interpretation; there is no certainty, no undeniable truth, no guarantee, no absolute.

The information found in this book will be disputed, inveighed against and much may already be obsolete. Any increase in knowledge and understanding can only help in the pursuit of greater knowledge and understanding. Of course, giving up the pursuit of knowledge may be the way to greater wisdom but the goal here is only to impart bits of information that the reader may not have encountered elsewhere and may find of interest. Wisdom is another issue altogether.

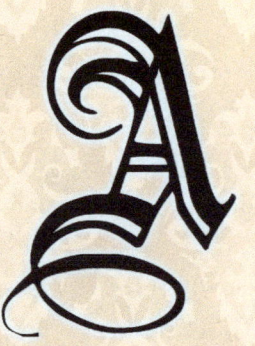

A B R A K A D A B R A
A B R A K A D A B R
A B R A K A D A B
A B R A K A D A
A B R A K A D
A B R A K A
A B R A K
A B R A
A B R
A B
A

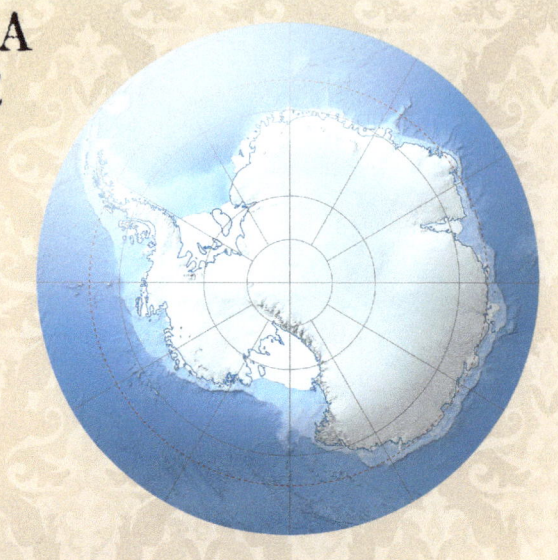

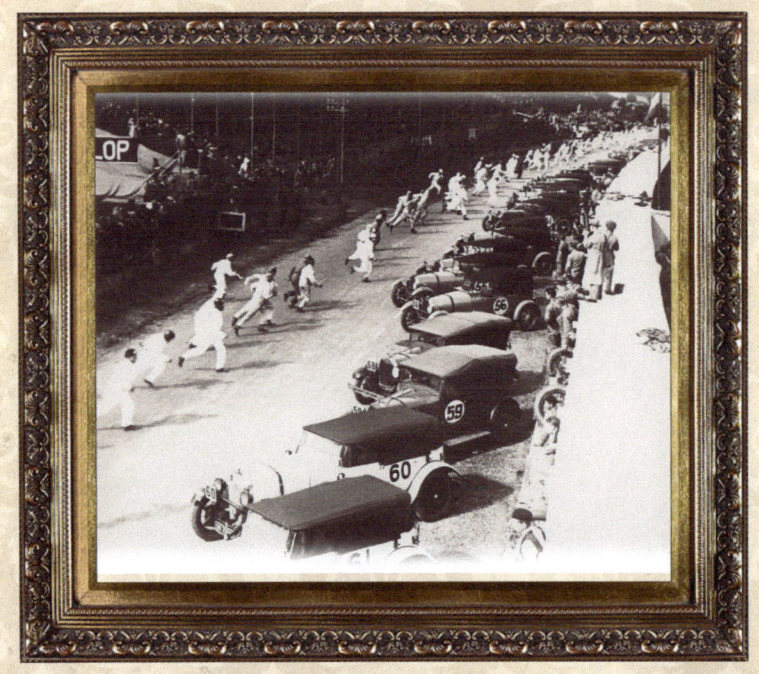

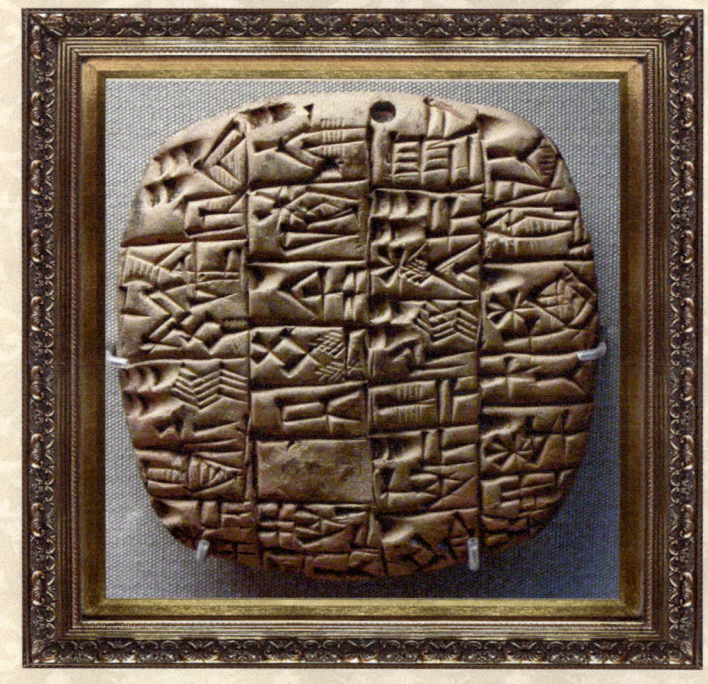

A. Did you know the word **açaí** is pronounced, ah-sa-EE?

Did you know the longest word in English beginning with A is **Antidisestablishmentarianism**?

Did you know that the Sumerians and the Egyptians developed their own forms of writing at about the same time, 3000 BPE? The Sumerians used tiny wedge-shaped marks impressed in wet clay tablets to convey ideas, concepts or objects, etc. These marks became increasingly abstract and when the Akkadians conquered the Sumerians they took abstraction even further, now that concepts such as justice and truth could be expressed in written form.

Alphabets:

Egyptian hieroglyphics were a more complex and expressive writing system that also developed shapes that represented sounds. These rudimentary alphabets, understood only by scribes and priests, were never taken to the next stage, an alphabet of characters that represented sounds. Various scripts, hybrids of hieroglyphics and cuneiform began to be used throughout what we now call the Middle East. Then some time, in that same area, someone or some persons, invented a true alphabet,* consisting of twenty some letters, combinations of which represented the sounds of the spoken word. As opposed to the over 600 cuneiform characters or the 6000 hieroglyphics, this alphabet could be written and read by even the least learned. The world has not been the same since.

Cool fact: The Arabic alphabet begins alif, bā; the Hebrew aleph, beth; the Greek alpha, beta; the Latin alphabetum, which gives us the English; alphabet. Most alphabets have less than 30 letters, the Armenian has 36.

*Just what alphabet was used on those tablets Moses brought down from the mountain, anyway?

Abracadabra:

We mostly know the word abracadabra as an incantation used by a stage magician to complete a magic trick. Amulets inscribed with the word, most often in an inverted pyramid where the last letter is deleted on each line until there is a single A at the bottom, were worn to ward off disease and such in the past. Abracadabra, while it may be the translation of an Aramaic word, has conflicting etymologies associated with it, leading to disagreement as to what it actually means.

Automobiles:

Did you know that an electric automobile held the land speed record until 1900?

Cool fact: In Dearborn, Michigan Henry Ford built a museum to house his collection of Americana. The museum covers 12 acres and contains an example of virtually everything ever produced in America plus items such as Abraham Lincoln's rocking chair and George Washington's campaign chest. In addition, the museum's grounds have a town consisting of the actual homes of famous Americans, 250 acres are covered with buildings where Thomas Edison, Abraham Lincoln, The Wright Brothers and Henry Ford among many others once lived or worked.

Antarctica:

You knew that Antarctica was cold but did you know the coldest temperature on record, minus 128.56 degrees F (minus 89C), was recorded there? You may have thought that only penguins lived there but in fact 1150 species of fungi manage to handle the cycles of freezes and thaws. Did you know the average thickness of ice in Antarctica is one mile? At one time, around 4.53 million years ago, Palm trees grew in the Antarctic.

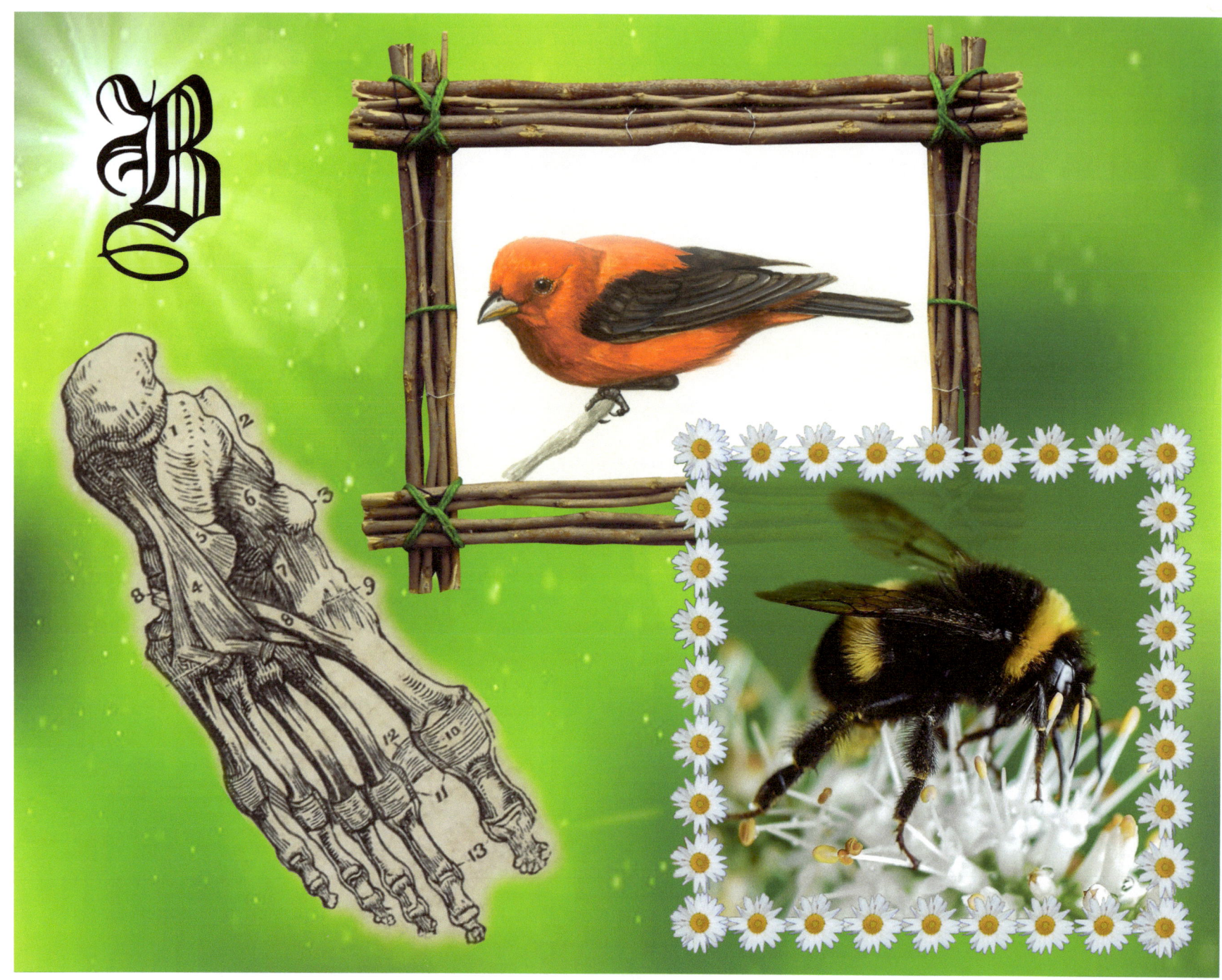

B. Did you know the longest word in English beginning with B is **Brachopsedo phemonoultra microscopis ilicovolcanoconiosis?**

The word has no spaces but it only ever appears broken into pieces.

Did you know that **bruschetta** is pronounced, broo-SKET-tuh?

Bach:

Did you know that J. S. Bach (1685-1750) learned the violin, played the harpsichord, was taught the organ by his uncle, Johann Christoph Bach, was known for his fine singing voice, became the church organist in Arnstadt, Germany and was composing, all before the age of eighteen? Bach spent his entire life directing music for churches, composing and performing.

He also became an expert in organ construction and was constantly called upon to test organs wherever they were built. His skill as a musician and composer were recognized during his life time, then suffered a decline in the following century when he was considered 'old fashioned.' But his genius received more and more appreciation as time passed.

The 'Saint Mathew Passion' has been called the greatest classical piece ever composed and much of his work remains in the classical repertoire. He fathered twenty children, some of whom also became renowned composers. Three of Bach's compositions, more than any other composer, were sent into space on the Voyager golden record.

Bones:

Did you know that a quarter of all the bones in the human body are in the feet?

Birds:

Did you know that birds have been on this planet for more than 140 million years? Between then and now it is estimated that there have been 2 million bird species. That number is now down to approximately 18,700 species. While new species do still show up, bird species are disappearing at an alarming rate.

Bird habitats are being destroyed as mankind exploits more of the land for the use of an ever-growing population. Almost everything that man does is detrimental to birds. Accidentally or deliberately we kill or injure birds by every means possible, (this applies to most every other form of life on the planet, too).

More than one third of the 800 U.S. species are endangered and one of their greatest threats is your kitty. It is estimated that cats kill more than 1 million birds *per day* in the U.S. alone. With the number of free roaming cats, currently around 150 million and rising, in the U.S., the call by environmental groups to keep kitty indoors takes on increasing urgency.

Cool fact: The Kakapo (Maori for "parrot of the night") is a large bird about the size of an Osprey. It is bright green and brown, can live to 80 and is endemic to New Zealand. There are only, as of 2015, 126 left alive.

Bees:

Now the Bees. Did you know that the annual average honey yield per bee colony for the year 2000 in the USA was 84lbs? The yield in the highest producing states was over 100lbs per colony. Consider then that a single bee, in its entire life, will produce one eighth of a teaspoon of honey! It's worth remembering that 30% of the world's crops and 90% of wild plants would fail without bees. Go easy with those pesticides!

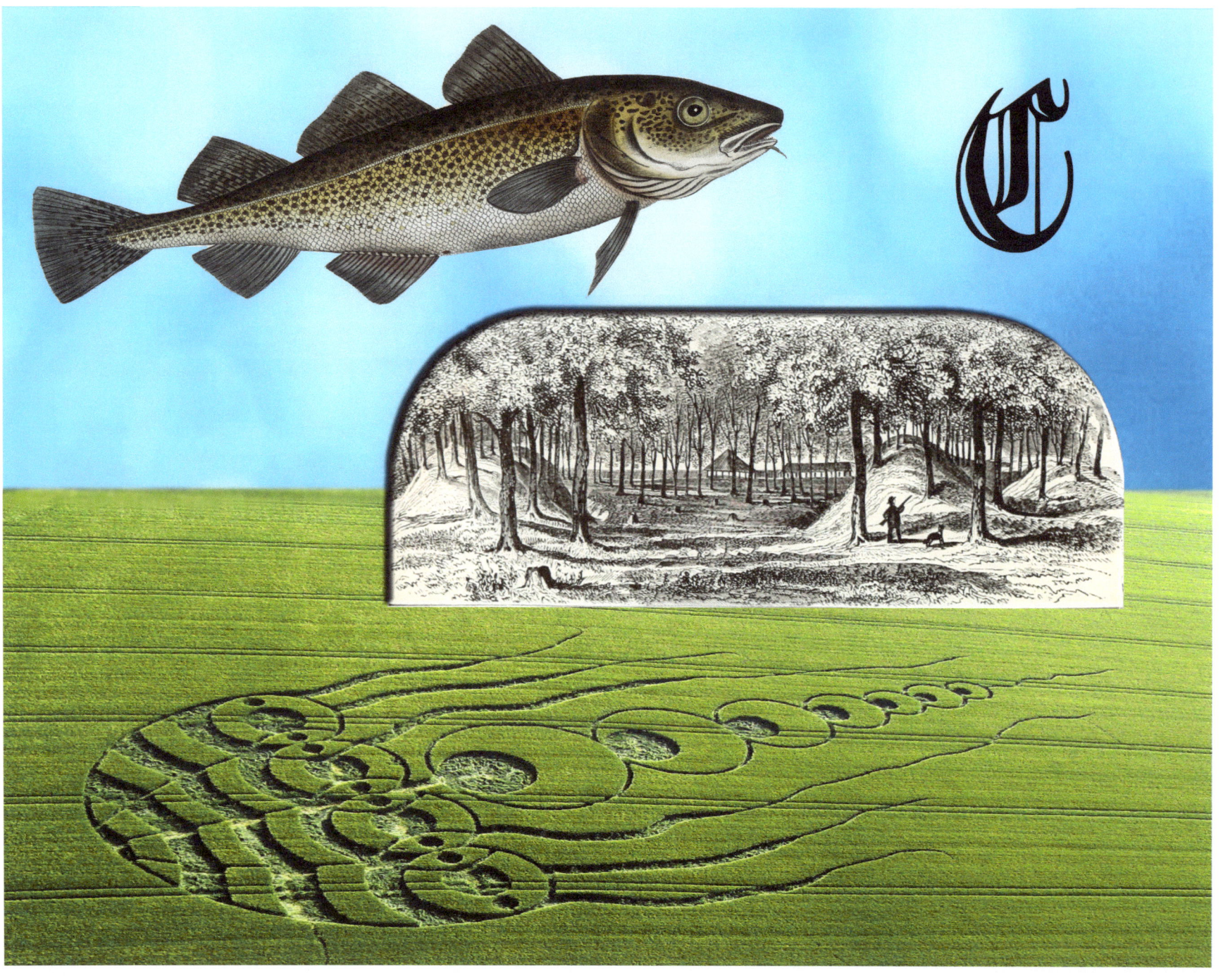

C.

Did you know the longest word in English beginning with C is **Counterproductiveness**?

Did you know that **charcuterie** is pronounced shar-koo-tuh-REE?

Did you know that **crudités** is pronounced, kroo-di-TEY?

Cahokia:

Did you know that around 1250 CE Cahokia, Illinois was home to 20,000 Mississippians? It was the largest city north of Mexico. Now hundreds of mounds and other structures, including the largest man-made mound in North America, can be visited at this 2,200acre historic site although some of the structures are now under modern houses and other constructions.

Climate Change:

Did you know that trees are crucial in the fight against Climate Change? A single tree can convert 48 lbs. of carbon dioxide, the poison we breathe out, into oxygen, what we breathe in. A single acre of some rain forests is home to 15,000 species.

Cod:

Did you know that Cod were once so prolific that at spawning time they could be scooped out of the water by hand? This cold, deep water fish which is usually found at depths of 260ft. on average, though 2000ft. is not uncommon, can grow to six feet in length and at one time was the predominant predator in its territory. The international market for cod started with the Vikings back around 800 CE. Many European countries got into it, then the United States and Canada established fisheries also.

The development of the eastern seaboard came about largely thanks to cod. By the 20th century, cod was endangered, having suffered a drop of 70%. Though this finding was disputed and the restriction of fishing was fiercely resisted, that over fishing has occurred is now generally accepted and catch amounts are monitored. To make up for the shortage of this popular fish, species that have cod in their name, as well as others that do not, like haddock and whiting, are now labeled and sold as cod.

Cool fact: The American revolution of 1776 in response to British tariffs was in part instigated by the "codfish aristocracy," a group which included John Hancock, who saw their illegal trade in contraband cod with the French Caribbean threatened by the measures England wanted to put in place.

Crop circles:

Did you know that Crop circles have been found in many countries around the world? While it has been determined that 70% were man-made, that still leaves a lot of room for those that attribute them to extra-terrestrials, electromagnetic forces, whirlwinds or other natural or unnatural forces to continue studying them. Like other phenomena that defy easy explanation, competing ideas come forward. Government cover-up and conspiracies, UFOs, fairies, take your pick. Any number of experts and/or wackos have their say. All very tantalizing, not too satisfying.

Cool fact: According to the Journal of Applied and Environmental Microbiology, something the Ancient Egyptians knew has been rediscovered. **Copper**, apparently, kills bacteria, viruses and infections by contact. Electrons from the bacteria, etc. are transferred to the copper which allows free radicals to attack the organism and kill the microbes.

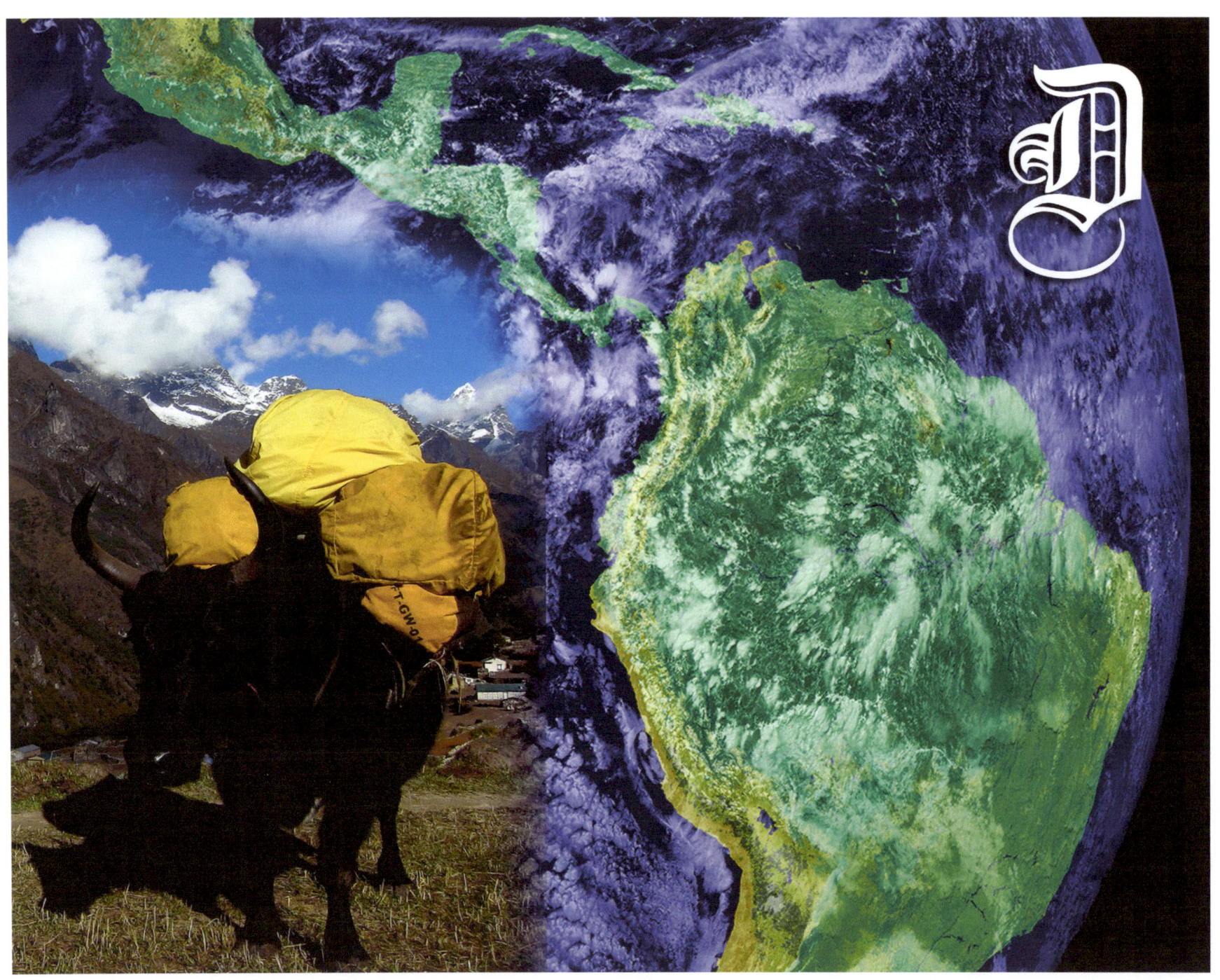

D. Did you know the longest word In English beginning with D is **Disproportionableness**?

Dzoh:

Did you know that a Dzoh, zo, dzho, zho is the offspring of a Yak and a domestic cow/bull? Technically a male hybrid is a Dzoh, a female is a Dzomo or Zhom. While the Dzoh are sterile, the Dzomo are fertile. Dzoh are used as pack animals in Tibet and in Mongolia, where the animal is known as a Khainag.

Dzoh are larger and stronger than Yak or cattle and are thought to be more productive in terms of milk and meat production. Generally, the offspring of the interbreeding of different species are infertile; like mules bred from a male horse and a donkey but where a donkey was the sire, fertile female mules are possible. Though not all animals can be crossbred in this manner, there are Ligers and tigons and Zonkeys. You can guess what they come from.

Doldrums:

Ever been in the doldrums, (inactive, mildly depressed, listless or stagnant)? Well, did you know the doldrums is what sailors called the area known as the ITCZ, the intertropical convergence zone? It circles the earth near the equator where the northeast trade winds meet the southwest trade winds. Moving back and forth across the equator these winds can result in heavy rains or dry, still weather that can last for days or weeks. Early sailing ships, before motors were invented, could find themselves stuck in the doldrums unable to go anywhere until the winds picked up again. It was not just boring but a real threat to the lives of those on board if supplies were low or if you needed to get somewhere in a hurry.

Deadeye:

Did you know that a Deadeye is a disc of hardwood with three holes that was used on sailing ships? Lanyards attached to shrouds pass through the holes in order to fastened and create tension on the shrouds holding up the masts. Although the block and tackle later replaced the deadeye, some sailing boats are using it again. It is said that the name comes from the fact that the deadeye resembles a skull.

Cool fact: The vaudevillian marksman known as Deadeye Dick was Bernie Dickson of Boerne, Texas. In 1907 at a competition in San Antonio, Texas, he fired at 72,500 two-inch blocks of wood tossed in the air and missed only nine of them.

Dutch treat:

Did you know that the term "Dutch treat" (to share the expense of a meal) was originally a way for the British to disparage the Dutch? In the seventeenth century, when the British and the Dutch were heavy military and trade rivals, in order to bolster their already strong sense of superiority, the British accused the Dutch of being cheap and sought to demean them in every way they could. A "Dutch concert" was discordant music, a "Dutch Nightingale" was a frog, "double Dutch" was gibberish and "Dutch courage" could only be attained by first getting drunk.

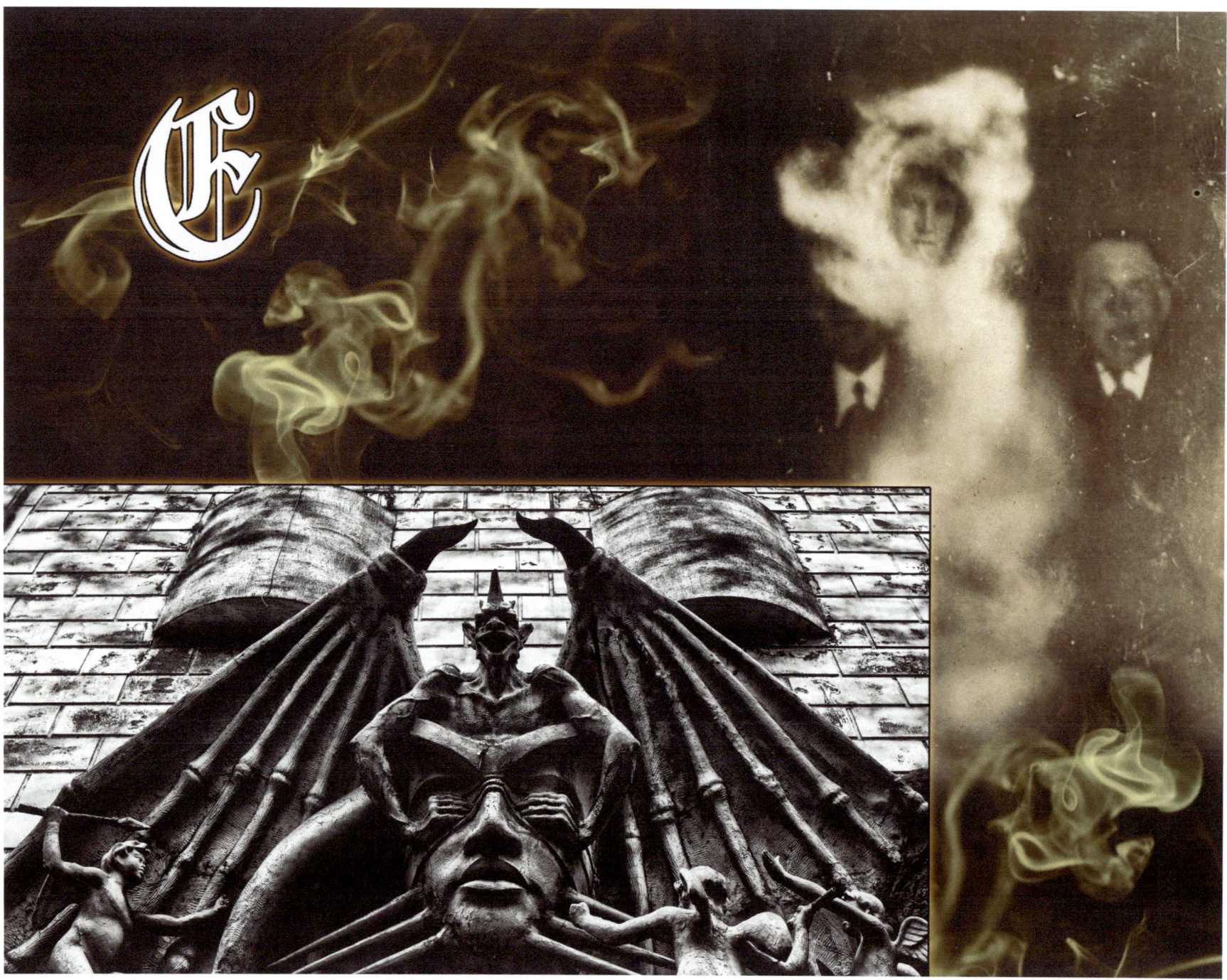

E. Did you know the longest word in English beginning with E is, **Electroencephalographic**?

Did you know that **espresso** is pronounced, ess-PRESS-oh?

Epsom salt:

Did you know that the naturally occurring mix of magnesium and sulfate known as Epsom Salt originally came from a bitter saline spring in Epsom, Surrey, England where the porous chalk Downs meet the non-porous London clay? Nowadays your Epsom Salts are just as likely to come from China. Epsom Salt cleans your bowels & your bathroom tiles. Got athletes foot? Toenail fungus? Epsom salt. Gout, sprains, bruises, blackheads, splinters, migraine headaches, hardening of the arteries? I could go on but as you can see it's good for a lot of things. It will even help your plants grow & keep your lawn green. Bright spots observed on the dwarf planet Ceres are consistent with reflected light from magnesium sulfate hexahydrate so if the spring in Epsom runs out we know where to find more.

Ectoplasm:

Did you know that in cell biology ectoplasm is the outer layer of the cytoplasm of a cell, endoplasm is the inner part but in the world of séances, mediums and the paranormal, ectoplasm was said to be a substance of "spiritual energy" that oozed from the body of a medium during a trance? It has been described in many different ways: as a 'viscous, gelatinous substance,' 'gauzelike,' 'a vaporous and fabric-like tissue' and as invisible! This is not surprising as a number of different materials including gauze, linen, paper and rubber were found to have been used during their sessions when investigators examined the techniques employed by certain "mediums" to deceive their customers and followers.

Evil:

I am tempted to combine E and F, for evil and faith. Why? Because so much of what we would describe as evil is carried out in the name of faith. Is there such a thing as evil? The amount of terrifying, bloodthirsty, deviant behavior that has been carried out by the most pious, well-meaning believers, from Popes to peasants, in the name of religion far exceeds anything done for pleasure or gain. Or from malicious intent, for that matter. The kind of madness that grips believers and drives them to diabolical ends is their devout adherence to what they understand to be absolute truth. Is this evil? We don't call madmen evil, the chemistry of the brain is not, we now understand, manipulated by some outside supernatural force. Those that slaughter, convinced they are carrying out the will of god, may well be deluded, but are they evil? The word evil is tossed around by those incapable of seeing that absolute convictions, unexamined beliefs, unquestioned rules and the tendency to obey regardless of the consequences is more likely to lead to unacceptable acts than disobeying orders ever will. People of faith, the more devout the better, fall most easily under the influence of fanatical leaders and will do the most horrendous things in the name of that in which they have faith. Is that evil?

English:

Did you know that English is the official language of nearly 60 sovereign states? It is the third most common native language in the world after Mandarin and Spanish. It is the official language of the United Nations and of the European Union.

Cool fact: For centuries the Lingua Franca of the Mediterranean area was a mix of words from those countries bordering the sea that traded with each other. Latin, French and Akkadian, having once been widely known outside of their country of origin, have, at different times in the past, been lingua franca. English is now the lingua franca most commonly used around the world.

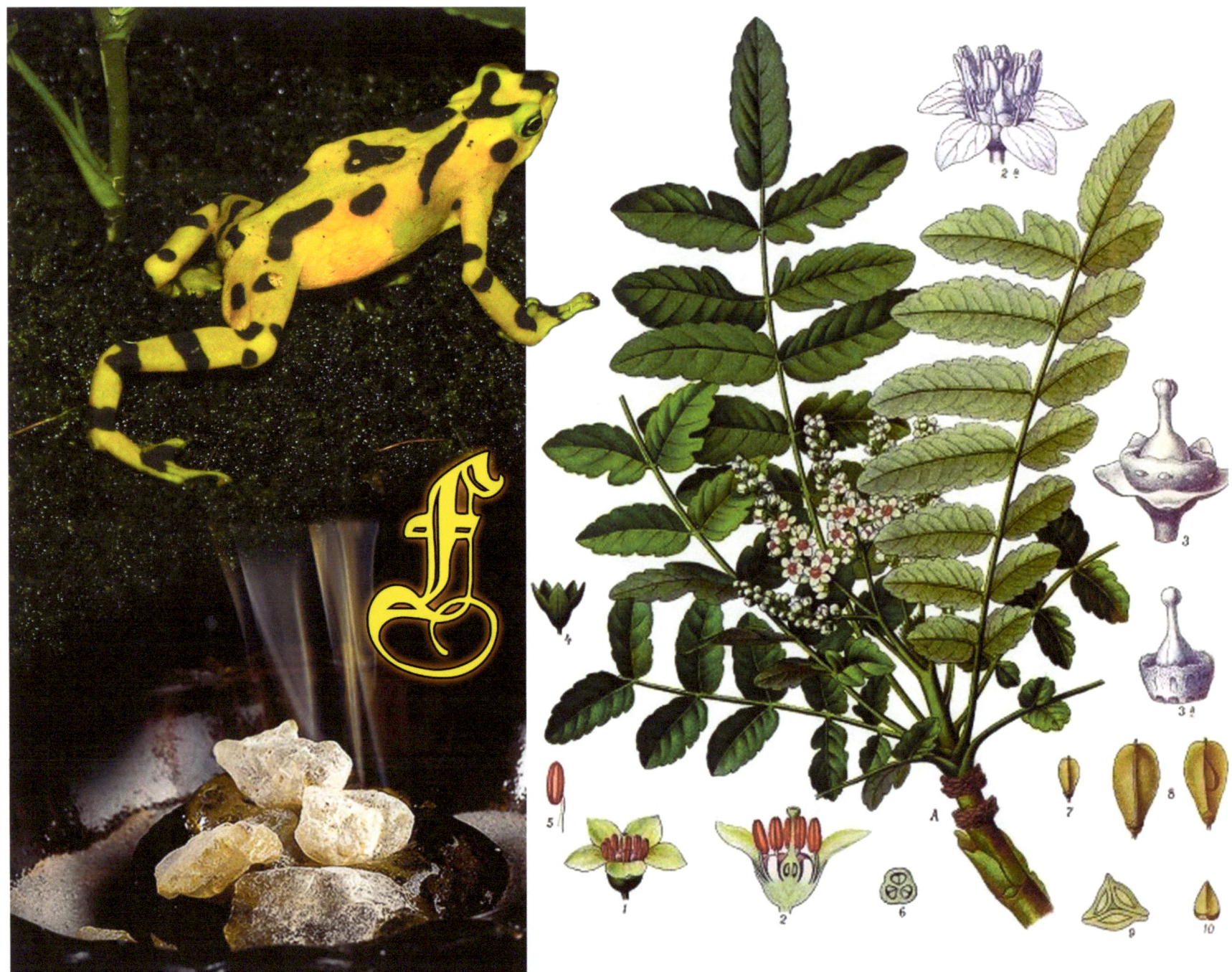

F. Did you know the longest word in English beginning with F is **Floccinaucinihilification**?

Did you know that **farro** is pronounced, FAHR-ro?

Did you know that **fungi** is pronounced- FUHN- jy?

Frogs:

Did you know that frogs have long been highly regarded in many parts of the world? In China the frog spirit Ch'ing-wa-Sheng is associated with healing and good fortune, and the noble money frog Chan Chu brings wealth and long life. In Egypt, the frog goddess Heget was a feature of the annual flooding of the Nile which brought out the frogs, symbols of life and fertility. The Celts saw the frog as lord over all the world. In Japan, it's a good luck charm for travelers. In the British Isles garden frogs, in every size and shape are a common garden decoration, they're seen as a symbol of good luck. A new species of frog, the Atlantic Coast Leopard Frog, was recently discovered on Staten Island, NY. The beautiful Golden Frog of Panama is actually a toad. The Chytridiomycosis fungus is wiping out many species of frog in Panama and the Golden Frog is, in addition, threatened by habitat loss, pollution and poaching. It may in fact already be extinct in the wild but much effort is being exerted to destroy the fungus so that captive bred frogs may someday be released back into the wild. Programs to educate people about the problems affecting the Golden Frog are somewhat effective but as the human population increases, this creature which ironically, is a symbol of good luck and prosperity may find itself out of luck.

Frankincense:

Did you know that Frankincense is made from the sap of the Boswellia tree? The sap is extracted from the bark then left to harden into a resin. The boswellia sacra grows in Africa and parts of the Middle East. It is considered Near Threatened by the International Union for Conservation. Though used mostly for incense, it is also distilled into an essential oil that has almost unlimited medicinal uses. If you have had a stressful day, a few drops of frankincense oil added to a hot bath will relax and rejuvenate you and help you get a good night's sleep. Since the smoke from burning frankincense is mildly euphoric and stimulating (and you thought it was the hymns and the stained-glass windows), it is classed by the World Health Organization as 'slightly hazardous.'

Feng shui: (FANG- sway) means 'wind and water'. Originally, before the invention of the magnetic compass, which was invented for feng shui, the Chinese relied on astronomy to determine the most beneficial alignment of houses and burial sites. For many thousands of years, the placement of structures followed the rules of feng shui, the aim of which is to choose a site that has good Qi (ch'i), Chee in English. Qi is the energy or life force pertaining to the area in question. Finding good Qi is similar to divining. A feng shui expert is hired to ensure that the best Qi is obtained at the site chosen for the undertaking. (Positive currents, those that carry the good qi, are known as 'dragon-lines' believed to follow the flow of underground water and the direction of magnetic fields beneath the earth's surface.) Over the centuries various schools of feng shui have developed to be used for particular purposes. Today, feng shui, once banned in communist China, is being used there again. In Hong Kong and Taiwan it has always been popular; in those countries and in the West, feng shui is employed by architects and interior designers to promote harmony and balance. Does it work? Try it and see.

Cool fact: The main gate of the Hong Kong Disneyland was shifted by 12 degrees during the planning stages due to feng shui considerations. This and other changes were incorporated into the architecture and design of the theme park to reflect the local culture.

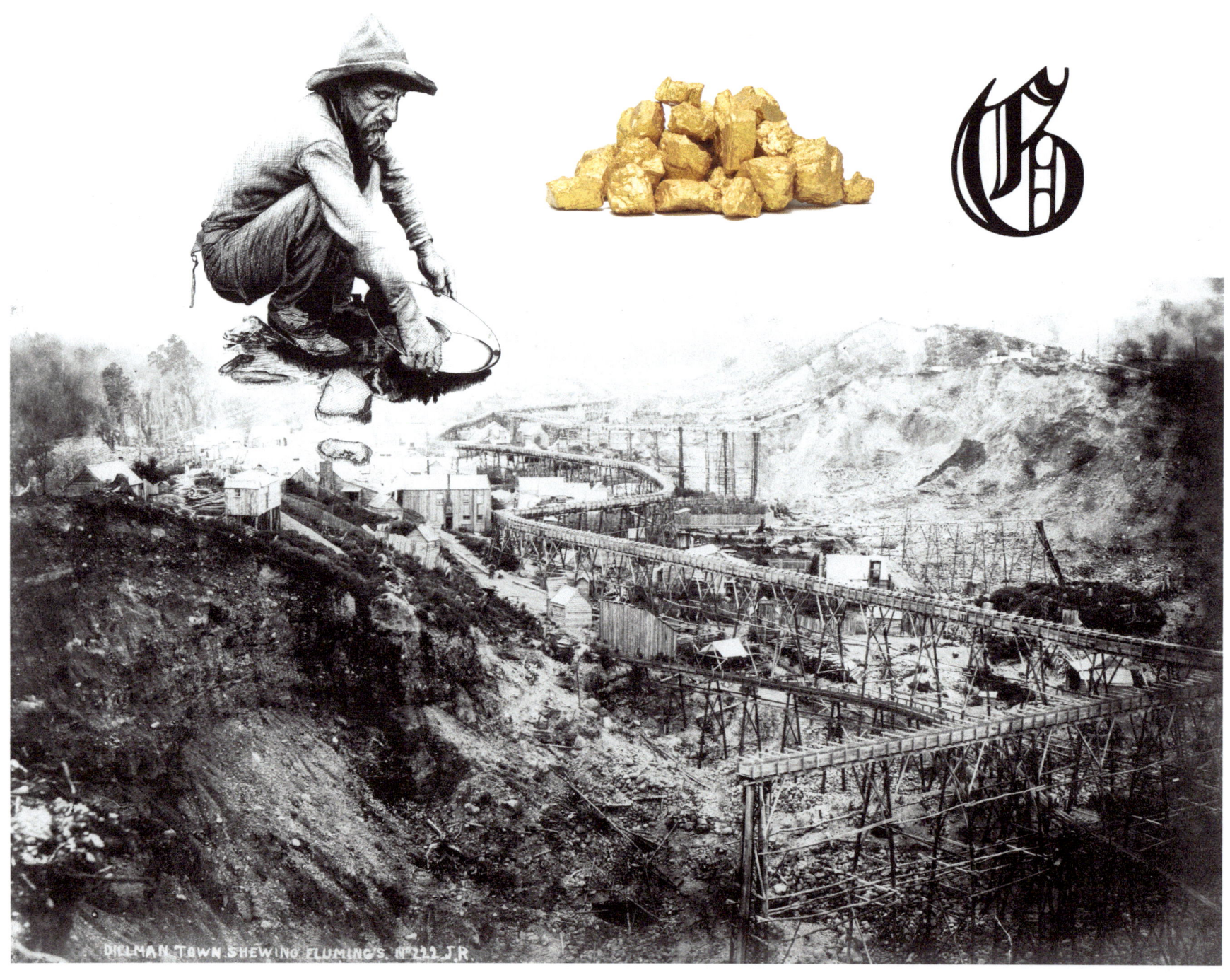

G. Did you know that the longest word in English beginning with G is **Gastroenterognastomosis**?

Did you know that **gyro** is pronounced YEER-oh?

Goose bumps:

Did you know that your mind and body are programmed to automatically react to fear, or emotions like love, awe, admiration, euphoria and to the cold? Goose bumps, which often accompany these emotions, are a result of the adrenaline rush that speeds up the heart rate in case you need to fight or run. It also causes the muscles attached to your hair follicles to contract, forcing the hair up. In animals with fur this reaction makes them instantly appear much bigger than they actually are and may be sufficient to give any would be attacker second thoughts. When it happens on porcupines, they not only look bigger but well-armed also. The erect hair also traps air which insulates against the cold. A bird's fluffed up feathers act the same way. In humans, the effect is most often observed on the forearms. Whether it is sufficient to keep you warm is debatable.

The medical term for goose bumps is *cutis anserina*, skin, goose. Many countries seem to prefer chicken or duck. In Spanish it's 'skin of a hen', Japanese, 'bird skin', in Chinese it's 'lumps on chicken skin' but goose skin is used in 15 European countries and Russia.

Horripilation is another term for the effect. The word, horror is derived from Latin, *horrere* which means "to bristle" and "be horrified" so, in the same way that "goose bumps" is named for the similarity to the skin of a plucked goose, chicken or duck, horripilation is the name for the hair reaction that accompanies this human reflex.

Cool fact: Music stirs the emotions and emotions stimulate the part of our brain called the hypothalamus. No one knows how emotions act on the brain this way or how music affects our emotions but when you get goose bumps listening to a piece of music you know it touched you.

Graphene:

Did you know graphene is the first two-dimensional material ever discovered? Under an atomic microscope it appears as a flat honeycomb lattice of hexagons. Derived from graphite, graphene has proved to be a most remarkable material with great potential. Scientists and researchers in a variety of fields are making discoveries that have resulted in the filing of thousands of patents. It may take a while but expect to see many products in the future that employ graphene.

Gold:

Did you know that the highest inhabited town in the world at over 17,000 feet is Rincoñada in Peru? It is devoted to gold-mining. The entire population (around 50,000) are either miners, their families or businesses that cater to their needs and the needs of the gold mining industry, refiners, assayers, buyers or wholesalers, all of whom are illegal or unlicensed and mostly unregulated. It is an environmental disaster area. Miners eventually succumb to silicosis if they are not killed or injured by roof cave-ins or explosions. Mercury poisoning, (mercury is used in the refining process) impacts everyone inside and outside the mines as the drinking water is contaminated whether it's source is snow, lakes, rivers or wells.

Around the world open pit mining, where 500,000 pounds of rock and ore might be removed to obtain a single ounce of gold, has created some of the worst environmental disasters. Mining rivers for gold, once done by individuals with gold pans, is now done with heavy equipment that might clear thousands of acres of forest in the process.

Do you really need that gold ring?

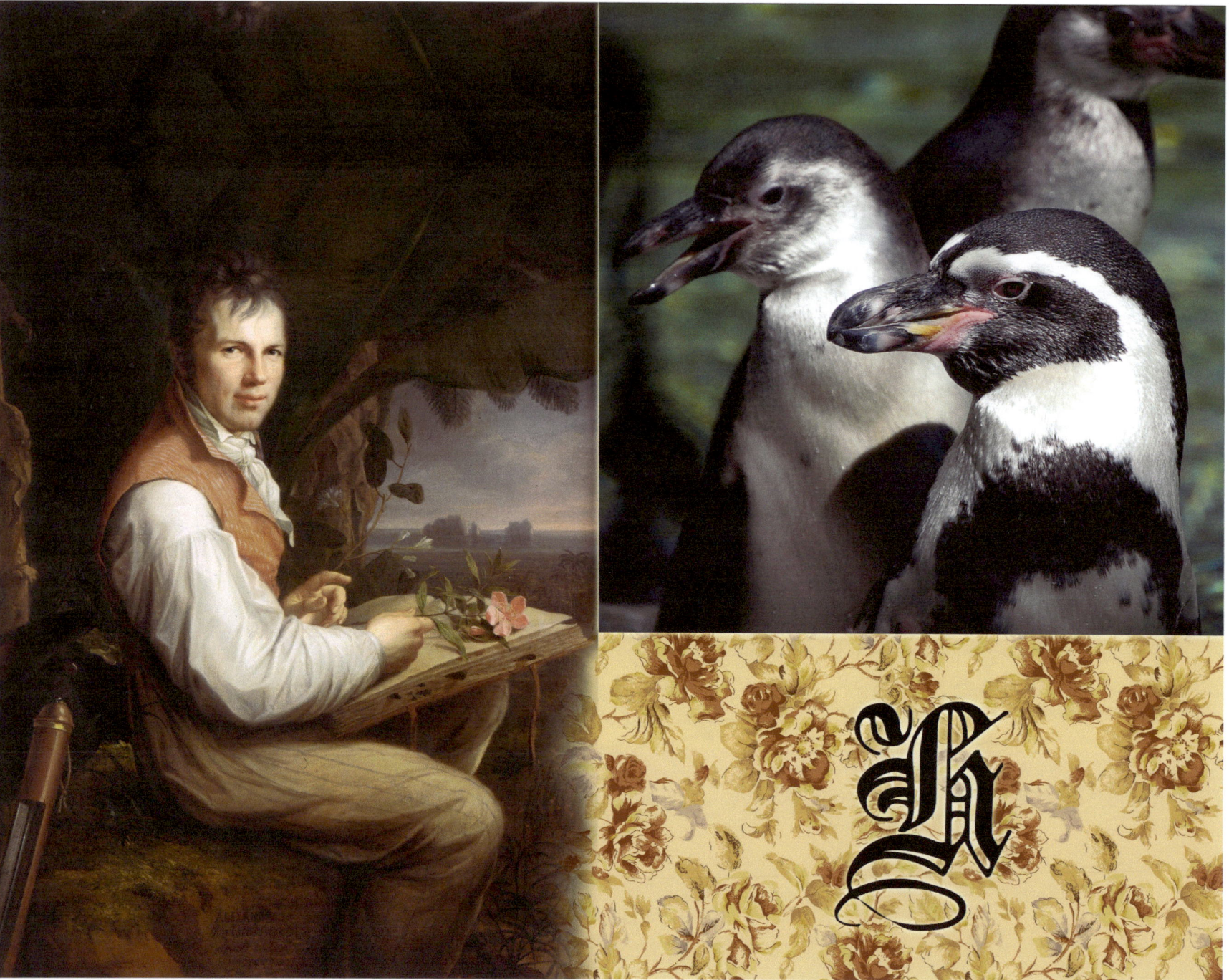

H. Did you know that the longest word in English beginning with H is **Hippopotomonstroesquippedaliophobia**?

Cool fact: This longest word in English means the morbid fear of long words.

History: His-tur –ree, His-tree

Did you know that in some languages history and story mean the same thing? Historians feel strongly that there is a big difference but history, at least in the past, was nothing but a story. It has been said that history is written by the victor, whose point of view is definitely biased. In fact, all written history will have a bias, whether because of the personal point of view of the writer or because the writer has an agenda; political, sociological, nationalistic, religious or racial. The information that an historian has access to, while being accurate, may also be biased and in complete contradiction to other reports. These and many other questions need to be addressed by the researcher.

Oral history when transposed to the written word will inevitably lose the emphasis and inflection of the spoken word. Translation of one language into another brings great opportunities for error. When two or three languages are involved, one or other of which may no longer have native speakers, the problems compound. There are also different schools of approach to history, each convinced that their method is the most reliable. This leaves the reader in a quandary: should one accept what one has read as the true history or seek out other versions? You have only to ask two different people to describe an event that happened yesterday to know that there is no such thing as the true story.

Humboldt:

You knew there was a Humboldt's current, right? But did you know there is a Humboldt's penguin, squid, skunk and over 100 other animal species? A Humboldt's Lily and 300 other plant species? How about minerals, rocks, Parks, forests, mountain ranges, rivers, waterfalls, a glacier, a bay, counties, towns and a crater on the moon? To name a few. Who is this guy, you might ask?

Alexander von Humboldt (1769-1859) was a naturalist. He traveled the world when it wasn't that easy to do and consequently saw and did things that few had done before and many that no one had ever done before. Everywhere he went he made notes, sketched, measured, mapped, experimented and tested; he once held electric eels in his bare hands to find out what kind of shock they were capable of giving (strong, it turned out!)

Humboldt's intimate knowledge of nature led him to the realization that the natural world was one unified organism. At a time when man was intent on subduing and destroying nature, he warned against the dangers of large scale agriculture, deforestation, and the disruption of ecosystems. Humboldt's work and writings had a great influence on thinkers and scientists. Let's hope it is not too late to see as he did, that unless we accept our place in nature, it may find that there is no place for us.

Hippopotamus:

In that vein, did you know that hippopotamuses or hippopotami, the second largest land animal, are endangered? They are being hunted for their meat and for their teeth which is being used as an alternative to ivory. The ecosystem where they live will be seriously affected if they become extinct and we as people will be the poorer for it. Find out what you can do to save wild animals and the environment.

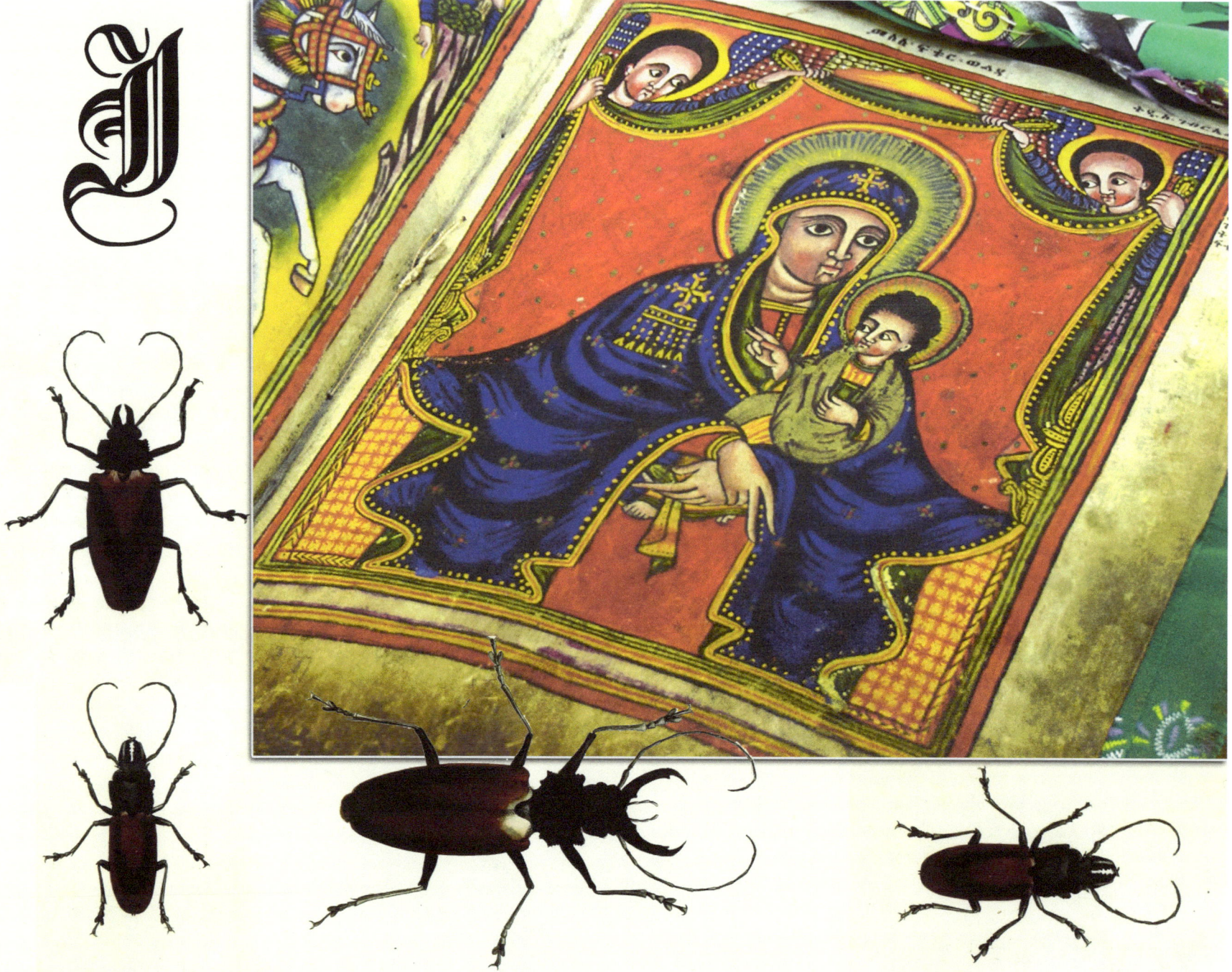

I. Did you know the longest word in English starting with I is **Incomprehensibilities**?

Intestines:

Did you know there are about 25ft. of intestines in your body? About 1,500 species of bacteria and flora live there. These microbes make enzymes to help you digest the food you eat, they produce hormones, and they help synthesize vitamins and clean up toxins as long as you help by eating a healthy diet.

Invasive species:

Invasive species are everywhere and getting rid of them might seem like an impossible task, especially when, having been in a place for any length of time, they might seem native. South Dakota's official State bird, the ring-necked pheasant, was originally imported from China. Did you know one country, New Zealand, has decided to eliminate invasives?

Mammalian predators, which the islands never had until humans brought them in, have caused the extinction of many endemic species, especially native birds. A number of smaller islands have been successfully cleared of rats, mice, stoats and rabbits. The two big islands, North and South New Zealand, present a huge challenge but the government, corporations, environ-mental groups and individuals are working separately and together to eradicate all non-native species from the country (the sheep too? I doubt that.)

Insects:

Did you know there are nine hundred thousand insects that have been named? Whether you are an entomologist or not there is still time for you to find and claim one for yourself as there are millions yet to be identified and named.

Icon:

Did you know an Icon, from the Greek Eikon, "image," once only referred to a religious painting of a saint found in Eastern Orthodox Catholic churches? People also hung them in their houses, generally of a saint for whom they were named or one that held special meaning for that family. Since certain saints were attributed with particular abilities, the icon would be prayed to. Over time certain icons gained the reputation for granting miracles, (if you prayed long enough for something and it came about, wouldn't you attribute it to the thing to which you had addressed your prayers?) Icons, similar to idols, are sacred religious objects but these terms are applied to iconic figures in society, idolized, hero-worshiped and yes, sometimes believed to perform miracles. The icon as symbol or sign that tells us what button to click or which restroom to use is an emblem, meant to communicate directly and simply, just like a church icon.

Ireland:

Cool fact: St. Patrick, born in England, was taken to Ireland as a slave when he was a boy. He escaped but returned after becoming a Christian. Why the absence of snakes in Ireland is attributed to St. Patrick having driven them out is unknown. According to the fossil record, there never were snakes in Ireland. To become a Saint the candidate has to have performed a number of miracles.

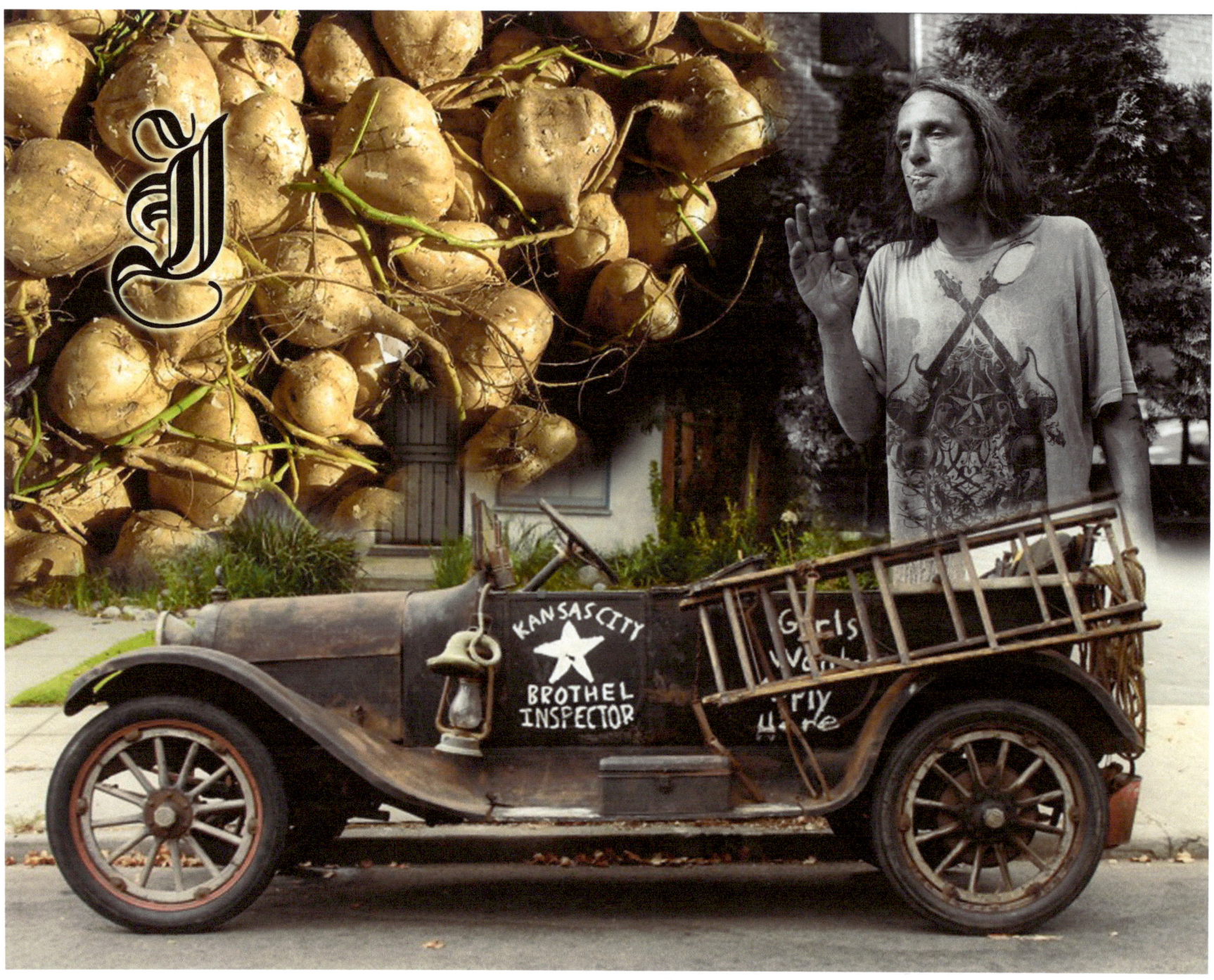

J.

Jalopy:

Did you know that your old heap, clunker, rust bucket, was known as a jalopy back in the 1920's? Though the American Heritage Dictionary says the word's origin is unknown, it is known that in those days old vehicles were shipped to Mexico for scrap metal. Freighters carried the metal out of New Orleans to Veracruz, just across the Gulf of Mexico. In order to identify their destination, the shipments had 'Jalap' scrawled on the side. Jalapa, or Xalapa, (pronounced Ha-la-pa) is the Capital of the State of Veracruz.

Jicama:

Did you know that jicama is pronounced, HEE-kuh-muh? The letter J, jota in Spanish, is pronounced, hoe-ta. Jalisco, jalapeno, jacal, jaguar and many other words from Mexico were translated from their original language into Spanish where X is often substituted for J, so we have Xico, *He-co*, and Mexico, *Meh-he-co* and Ha-lap-a, Xalapa. Jicama is a tuberous root native to Mexico usually eaten raw with lime juice and chili but also in salads or cooked. Only the root is edible the rest of the plant is poisonous

Joint:

Did you know that holding onto a marijuana cigarette for an extended period or not sharing the "Joint" with others is known as "Bogarting"? Humphrey Bogart usually had a cigarette dangling from his lip, (he died of lung cancer) though one would never share a tobacco cigarette. Smoking marijuana is more of a communal activity and it has been likened to the sharing of the peace pipe among Native Americans. The fact that there was less of it to go around might be a more plausible explanation. It will be interesting to see if the practice of passing the joint continues once marijuana is legalized and everyone can have their own stash.

Joke:

Did you know that the first recorded joke is Sumerian? Writing originated there, and yes, it's a fart joke. It's actually a proverb, (we will examine proverbs under P) more than 3900 years old. It goes, "Something which has never occurred since time immemorial, a young woman did not fart in her husband's lap." There is an Egyptian joke from 1600 BPE and the oldest English joke dates from the 10th century PE. None of them are particularly funny but they do contain the ingredients of most jokes to this day: sex, bodily functions and play on words.

The question and answer format remains popular: "Why did the chicken cross the road?" Riddles, racism, taboos and puns that are often intended to embarrass or are made at the expense of the listener still fill the repertoire.

Knock, knock jokes involve the audience more than some but all require some participation or at least a reaction. The audience is set up for the 'punch line' which will often have a conflicting meaning that they 'get' and see the humor therein. This will evoke laughter or groans. As the ratio of lawyers to regular citizens continues to increase, presumably so too will the amount of lawyer jokes:

A rich old lady called her lawyer to make out her will. In his most sympathetic and reassuring manner he said, "Now don't get all upset over this, just leave it all to me." "I might as well." The lady sighed. "You'll get it anyway."

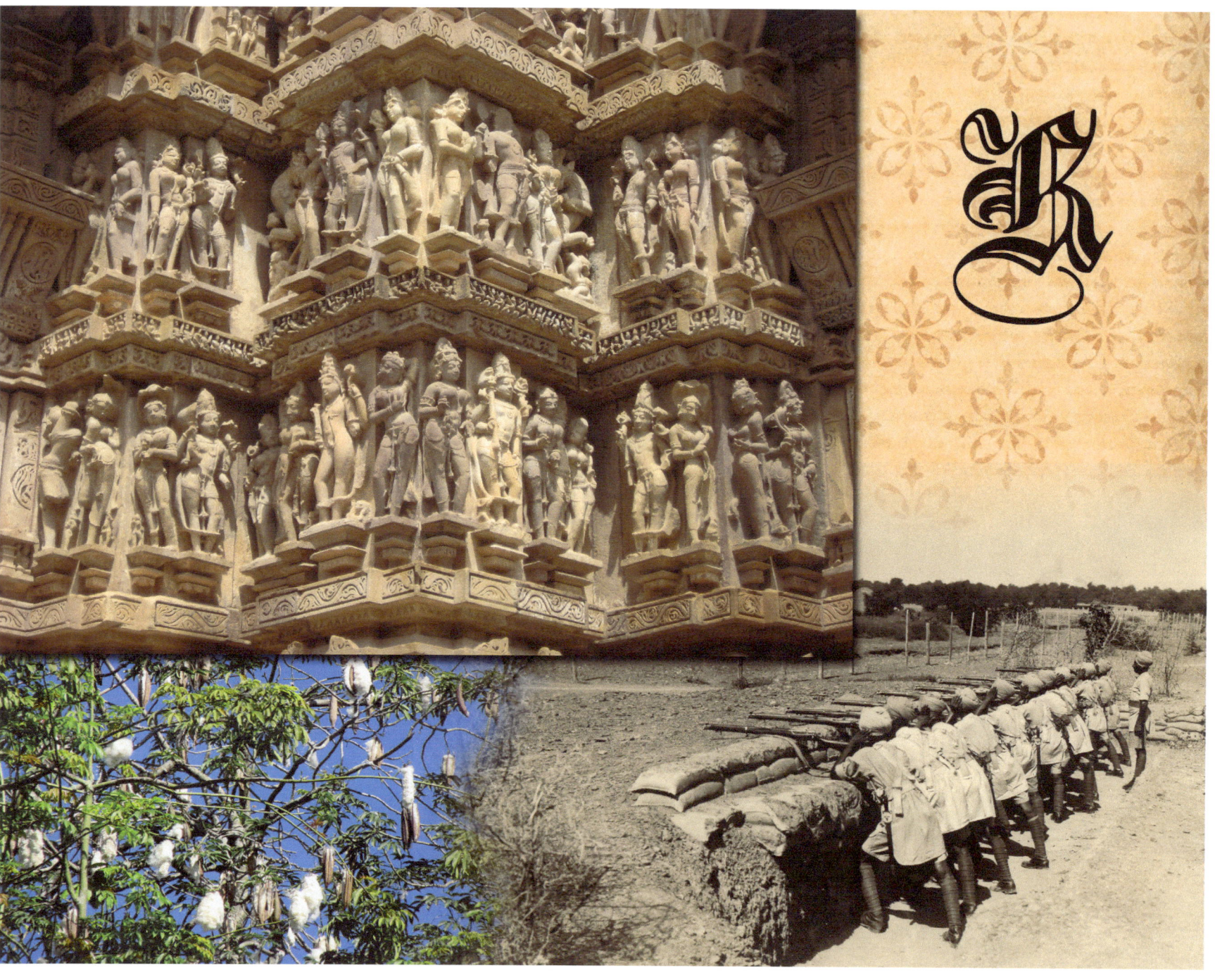

K.

Khajuraho:

Did you know that the Khajuraho group of Hindu and Jain temples built between 950-1150 CE in Mahya Pradesh, India, now a UNESCO world heritage site, once had a total of 85 temples, about 20 of which have survived? Carved from a fine local sandstone, the intricately carved scenes of daily life, mythical personages and animals are very detailed. It is estimated that the work required hundreds of highly skilled sculptors to produce the several thousand images. Put together with mortise and tenon joints, using no mortar, the stones are held in place by gravity. Desecrated and mutilated by invading Muslims in the 14th century, these finely wrought sculptures continue to impress. Though most famous for the erotic depictions of every kind of sexual intercourse, those scenes represent less than 10% of all the sculptures that cover the buildings inside and out.

Kapok:

Did you know that Kapok is the fluffy material attached to the seeds of the Ceiba tree that, like the dandelion, carries the seeds on the wind to new places to grow? Kapok was used in life vests as it is extremely water resistant and stays buoyant for hours. When the supply of Kapok to the USA was cut off in WWII, the fluff of cattails was substituted and was found to provide even better buoyancy than Kapok. Both have been used as padding in armor, mattresses and pillows. The Ceiba tree grows to 230 feet tall and provides lots of other useful products.

Khaki:

Did you know that Khaki comes from Urdu and means, 'soil colored'? William Hodgson, second-in-command of the Corps of Guides, a regiment of Indian soldiers in the British India Army formed in 1846, commissioned his brother in England to send uniforms for the Corps to wear. Initially called 'drab' it became known as khaki when the material started to be made locally and was dyed with mulberry juice to produce the color known familiarly as khaki around the world.

Bruce Chatwin in his essay, "Shamdev: the wolf-boy", writes of a man, "dressed in *white* hand-woven khaki cloth." Could it be that the cloth itself was/is known as khaki before it was/is dyed, 'khaki'?

Koko:

Did you know that the sound, feel, color, packaging and your memory associations have as much to do with how you respond to things you eat as do your taste buds? Manufacturers commission neuroscientists to determine the best way to get you to buy their product. Lab tests have shown that some brands fail due solely to the color of the package. For instance, Coca-Cola's white can, introduced in 2011 to raise funds for polar bears, had drinkers convinced that the company had altered the taste of the cola; they had not. A brand of milk-chocolate truffles called Koko may have failed because it was found that the hard K sound is associated with bitterness. Maybe that's why little Johnny won't eat his Kale. Kill and the KKK don't sound so good when you think about, do they?

Cool fact: Although the letter K appears in the Spanish alphabet it is only used in words borrowed from other languages.

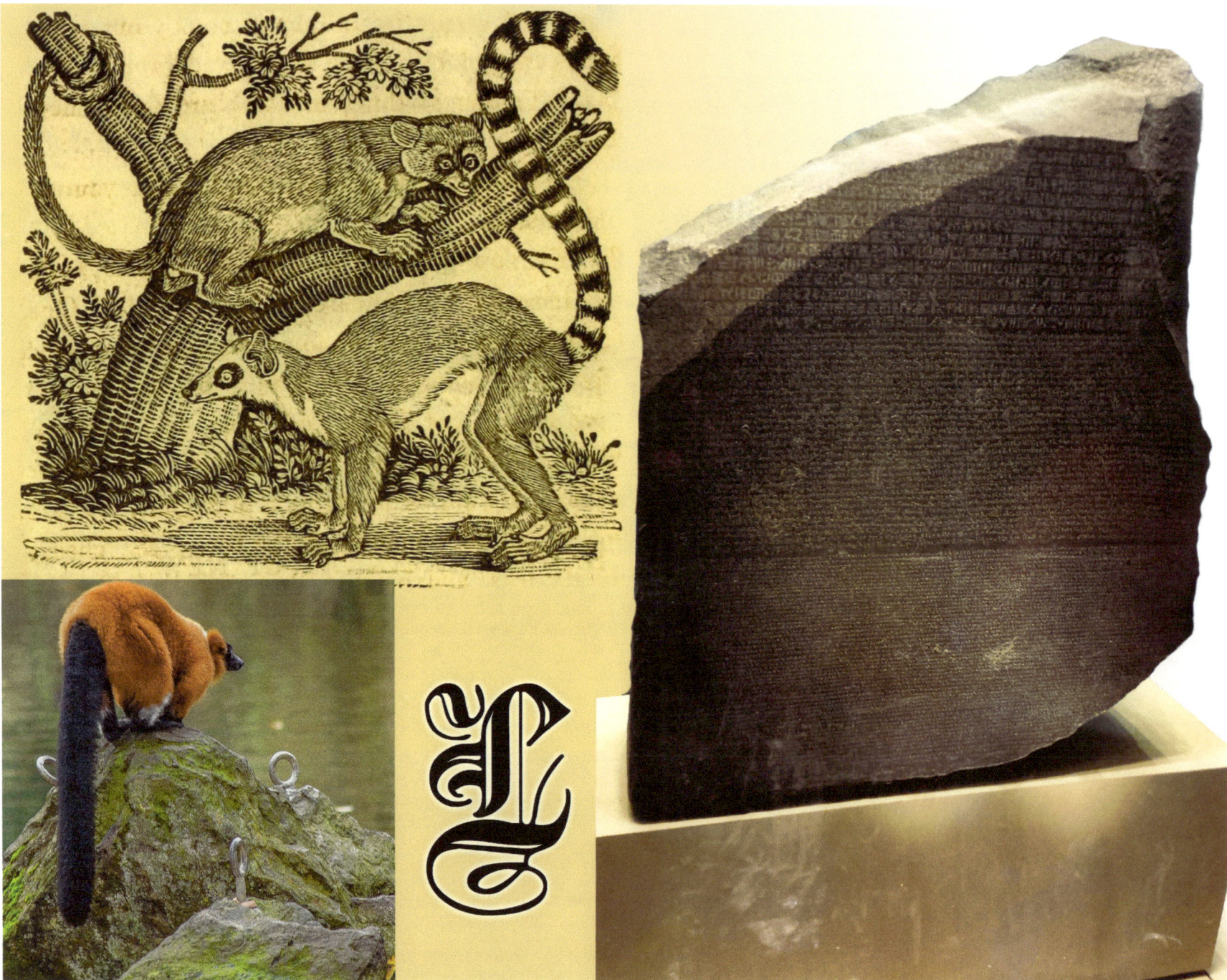

L.

Lemuria:

Did you know that Philip Scather, noticing similarities in the flora and fauna of Madagascar to those in India and Africa, concluded that Madagascar was the last existing portion of a lost continent he called Lemuria, that had sunk below the Indian Ocean? Why Lemuria? Because of the lemurs on Madagascar. Once tectonic plate geology was understood, that theory took a dive but just like Atlantis or the island of Mu, Lemuria has not been allowed to die and like them, has been placed in the Atlantic, or the Pacific. The search goes on. Scather was almost right, however, as Madagascar and India were once part of the same land mass which broke apart millions of years before there were lemurs.

Luminescence:

Did you know there are more than twenty kinds of luminescence with names like Crystalloluminescence (produced during crystallization), Photoluminescence, Piezoluminescence, etc.? Bioluminescence is the result of biochemical reactions in living organisms. Notable examples of bioluminescence are fireflies and glowworms. Armirillaria or the honey mushroom and the mycena mushroom, of which there are thirty-three species, emit bright flashes known as foxfire. Dinoflagellates in fresh and sea water, (mostly plankton but there are thousands of different kinds) cause luminescence under the surface of the water.

You can enjoy the experience of scooping luminescence into the air. Unfortunately, certain dinoflagellates, blooming under certain temperature or salinity conditions, are responsible for red tides which kill fish and shellfish and cause eye and throat irritation in humans.

Languages:

Did you know that as of this year, 2018, there are 7097, or 7,102, the number is constantly in flux, living languages in the world? Many languages became extinct as the native speakers were either killed by diseases imported by invaders or by the invaders themselves. Genocide continues but globalization and urbanization are the main reason that languages are now disappearing. When fewer people are speaking it and their children are not learning it, a language is said to be "endangered." Some known as "dormant" languages are still in use but only for ceremonial or symbolic purposes. Although there have been new languages invented, Esperanto and Klingon, for instance, the disappearance of languages is of great concern. The understanding that much of the history, knowledge, beliefs and identity of a People is embedded in their language has resulted in conscious efforts to maintain or renew its daily use, although this is usually restricted to the few. In some circles it is believed that there are advantages to having one world language, that the ability to communicate easily would make for less conflict and xenophobia. Unfortunately, this has not been found to be the case.

Cool fact: The few languages in the world that can't be shown to relate to any other include Basque, Zuni, Purepécha of Mexico and Ainu of Japan.

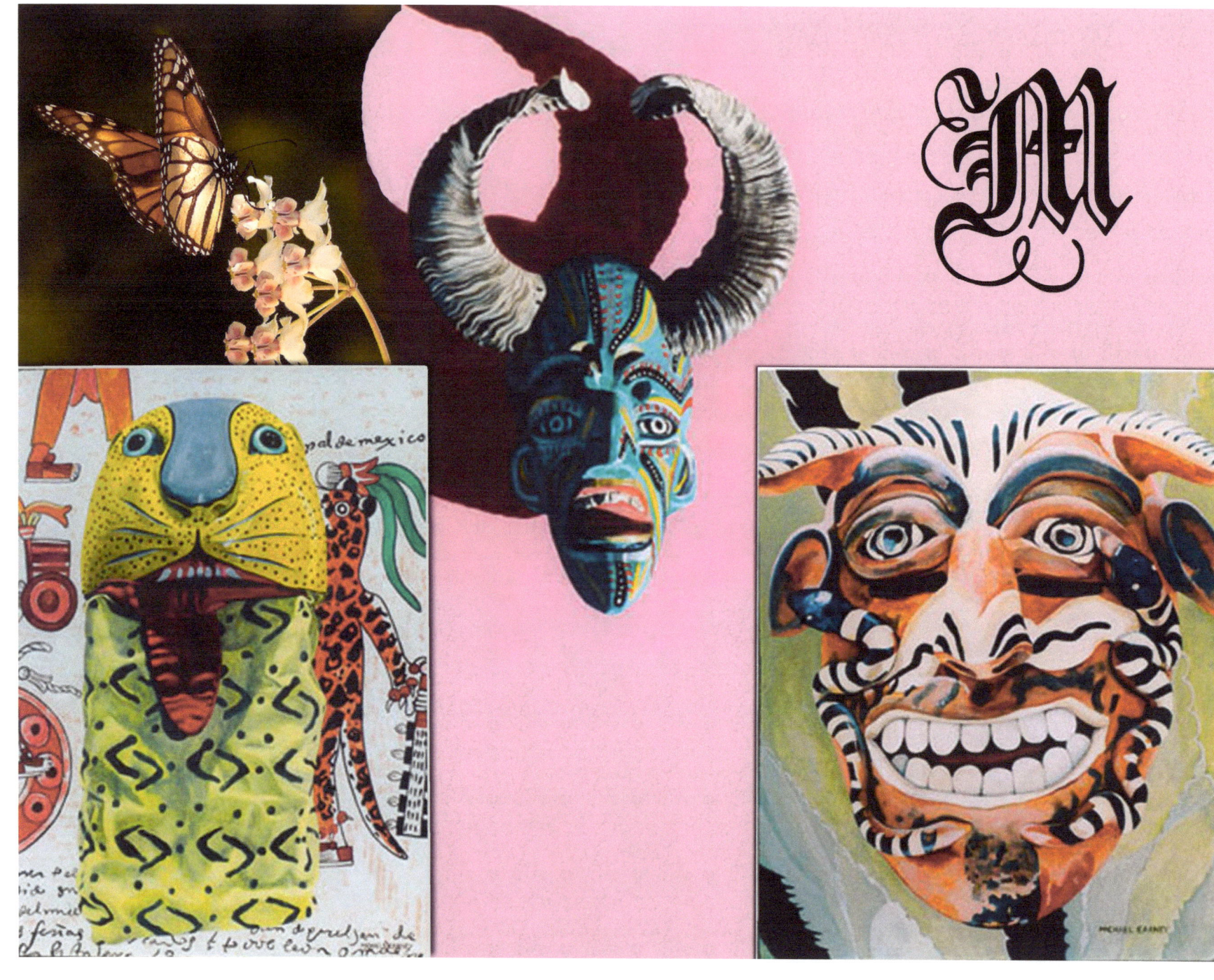

M. Did you know that if there were no **Milkweed** there would be no **Monarch** butterflies?

Monarch Butterfly:

In the spring Monarchs, heading north from their wintering grounds in Mexico, mate and die after they cross the border, but not before the female lays her eggs on the leaves of the milkweed plants that have just come up. Successive generations of monarchs make their way north as far as Canada, repeating the process as they find milkweed along the way. Most of the monarchs that "return" to Mexico for the winter have never been there before! If those that are attempting to eradicate the milkweed are successful and the grasslands where it grows are all developed, they will have eradicated not only the plant but the monarch butterfly, too.

Masks:

Did you know that Masks have been used by Mankind for many thousands of years? A 7000year-old stone mask in the Biblical Museum in Paris, France is the oldest known but cave paintings depicting figures wearing masks date back 30,000-40,000 years. Throughout history almost every society in the world has used masks for communing with the gods or nature spirits, curing, war or entertainment. The Spanish mask tradition, (Hernan Cortez had the newly created masked play "Moros y Cristianos" performed shortly after arriving in Mexico) melded easily with the traditions of Mexico and continues to play an important part in religious dances and fiestas. The famous Mexican wrestler "El Santo" continued to wear his mask after he retired and was buried wearing his silver 'Lucha Libre' mask, continuing the death mask tradition of the Aztec and Mayan rulers. Although the magnificent mask carvings of the tribes of the Pacific Northwest are now made as art objects or for retail sales, the elaborate Katchina masks of the Zuni and Hopi in New Mexico are still used in tribal ceremonies. In festivals around the world, from Japan to Alaska, masks play an important role. The Latin word 'persona' which we use to mean our self, the self we project to the world, means mask. It is the image we choose to present to others, how we wish to be known. Masks, in fact, allow us to behave in ways we could not normally. The person portraying the god whose mask he wears becomes the god, Bruce Wayne becomes Batman, and unmasked, the Lone Ranger is no longer the Lone Ranger. The clown needs only his red nose to behave in the most outrageous, silliest, and unconventional ways possible.

Marijuana:

Did you know that Marijuana, produces a fine oil than can be used as a lubricant or as fuel? Like so many under-utilized 'weeds' It can be made into clothing, rope, paper; the seeds are nutritious and it has a variety of medicinal properties. It is high in omega-3 and is widely prescribed for PTSD and other ailments. Used for thousands of years, it was made illegal in the USA in 1937 thanks to the efforts of Harry J. Anslinger, the director of the newly created Federal Bureau of Narcotics. Although many European countries are attempting to have marijuana reclassified, their efforts are being stymied by the Single Convention on Narcotic Drugs to which all belong. Several countries, mostly those with Moslem populations, still impose the death penalty for possession of marijuana.

Mount Everest: Named for Sir George Everest is, at 29,029 feet or 29,035 feet above sea level, according to whom you ask, is considered the world's highest mountain. Now the Chinese, Tibetans and Nepalese are fighting over naming rights but "Holy Mother Mountain" appears to be winning. However, its claim as the highest mountain is also being contested. Mauna Loa and Mauna Kea on the island of Hawai'i are considered the "tallest" since, starting on the sea floor, they have more height than Everest. Then, Mount Chimborazo in Ecuador offers another challenge. Situated at the equator, (Ecuador in Spanish), Chimborazo rises higher than any point on earth because the world bulges at the equator.

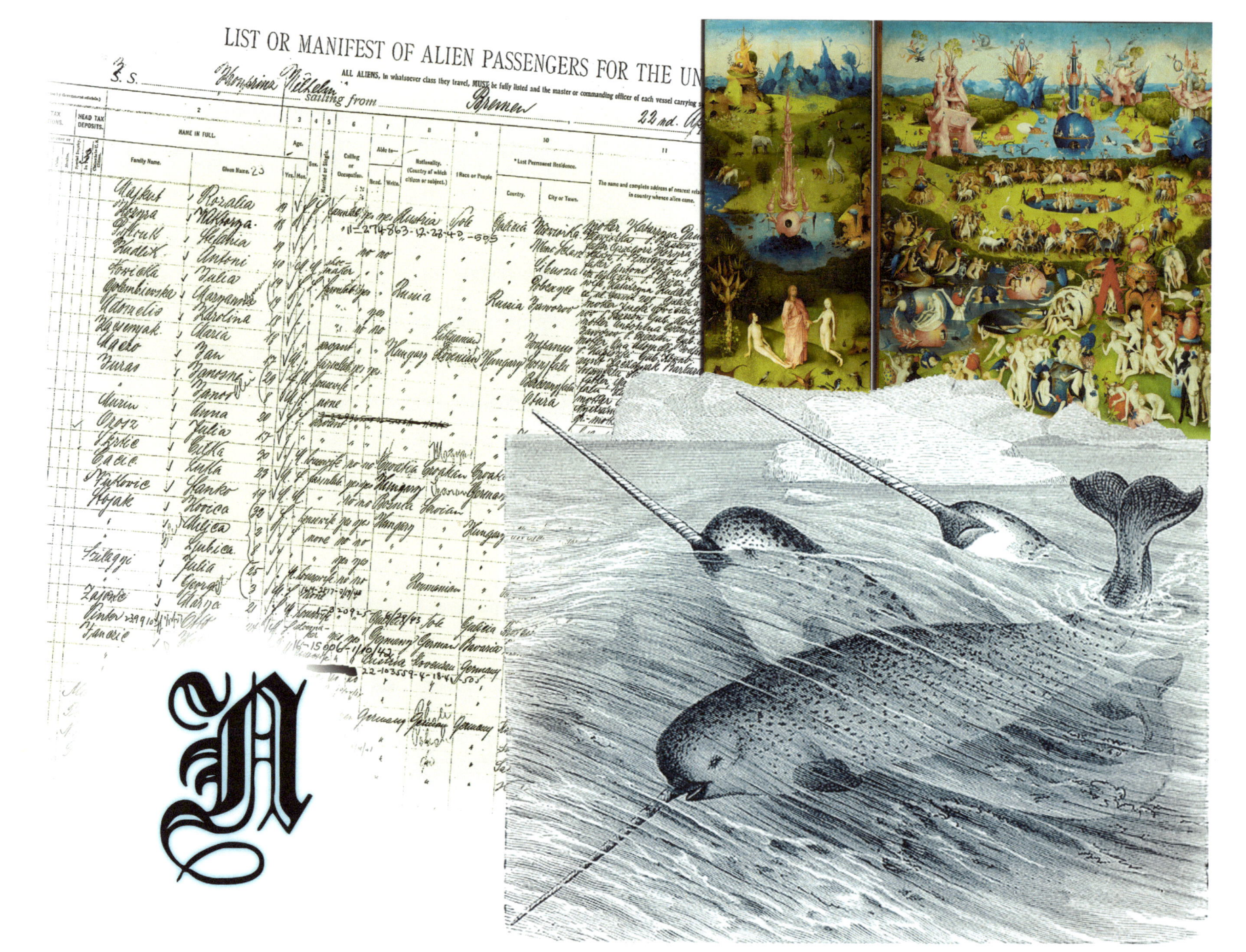

N. Did you know the longest word in English starting with N is **Nitrochloroanthraquinones**?

Did you know that niçoise is pronounced, nee-SWAHZ?

Narwhal:

Did you know that the "tusk" of the Narwhal is actually a canine tooth that protrudes through its upper lip? The Narwhal and the Beluga whale are the only two living members of the monodonidae species. It lives in the arctic seas, grows to 13' or 18', lives up to 50 years, can dive to a depth of 4900' and stay under water for 25mins.

The tooth, which has earned the Narwhal the name, 'unicorn whale,' grows in a spiral up to 10 feet in length. It is soft on the outside and hard on the inside. Although there are a number of theories, it was not known what the tooth was for until very recently when it was determined that it is a sensory organ, registering temperature changes and the presence of chemicals in the water; it is extremely sensitive to any changes in the surrounding environment.

The Narwhal is now a Near Threatened species in part due to seismic oil exploration surveys which disrupt the animals' migratory patterns and climate change. Less ice means greater vulnerability to hunters. The Inuit people are allowed a regulated subsistence hunt. Their catch has increased with the increased exposure. One ounce of Narwhal skin contains as much vitamin C as one ounce of orange juice, and it is surmised that the Inuit of the past would not have survived without it.

Names:

Did you know that last names only came into existence about a thousand years ago? As populations grew, simply saying 'John' wasn't enough. John's son Philip or Philip Johnson helped, then 'John the Miller' or John Miller came about. Fletcher, Wheelwright, Baker, Piper and the like came to be the name of those that plied that particular trade. Alternatively, their place of origin might be attached: London, Beach, Rivers, etc.

In the United States of America many names were invented by immigration officials at Ellis Island as non-English speaking and often illiterate immigrants arrived. Even if they could spell their name in Cyrillic or some other alphabet, that didn't help the hard-pressed officer trying to process the thousands of arrivals. He might take what he heard the immigrant say and render it as best he could into English.

African slaves were known by the name of their owner for much the same reason although probably they were never asked their Swahili or native name. As generations of slaves were traded or sold they might retain the name of their previous owner or adopt that of their new one. If you are a black American named Fitzgerald, for example, tracing the ancestry of your name back to Scotland is not going to help very much genealogically.

Cool fact:

The Dutchman Jeroen van Aken dropped Aken (his ancestors came from Aachen in Germany), took the name of the town where he was born, s'Hertogenbosch, Latinized his first name and became, Hieronimus Bosch (1450?- 1516), painter. One of his most known paintings is *The Garden of Earthly Delights* which hangs in the Museum del Prado in Madrid, Spain.

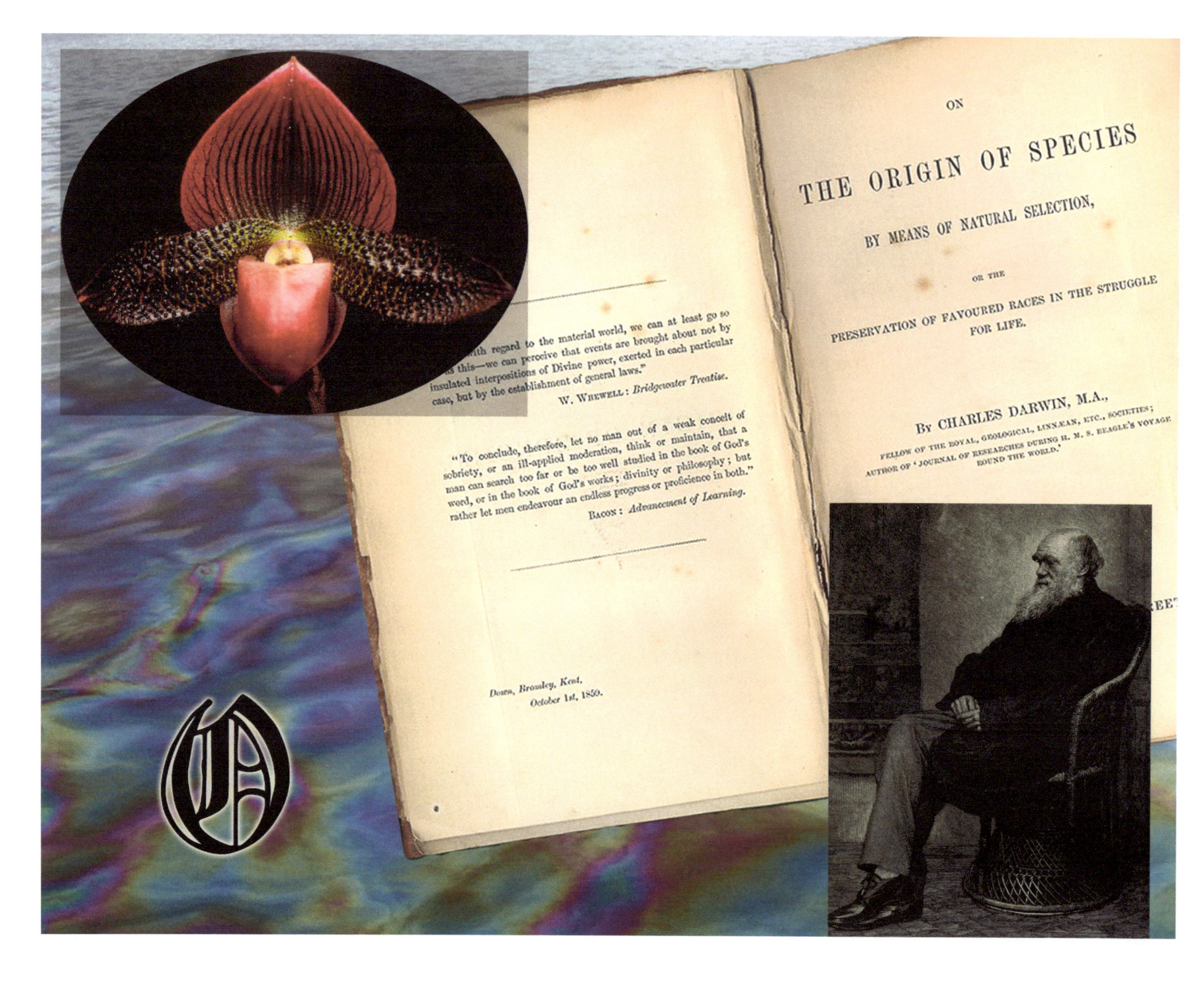

O. Did you know the longest word in English beginning with O is **Organophasphorus**?

Origins:

Did you know that Charles Darwin had his basic theory of natural selection by 1838 but it wasn't until twenty years later that he decided to publish *The Origin of Species, or the Preservation of Favoured Races in the Struggle for Life*? Over the centuries possible explanations for the diversity of life and how little evidence for the belief in Intelligent Design there was had been put forward. After his mind-expanding trip on the *Beagle* Darwin pulled all the evidence for natural selection together, then set it aside.

Meanwhile, Alfred Foster Wallace was coming to the same conclusions on the other side of the world. The package that Darwin received from Wallace in 1858, laying out *his* theory, convinced Darwin that he had to get his version out or it would be eclipsed. the Linnean Society which is dedicated to the dissemination of information on natural history, presented both of their papers at one of their meetings, arousing very little response, (except from Patrick Mathew, a gardener who had published his similar theory the same year Darwin left on the *Beagle*).

Darwin published, "The Origin" in 1859 and continued to make revisions through the sixth edition which was published shortly before his death.

Orchid:

Did you know that according to the 2013 world checklist, there are 27,135 naturally occurring species of Orchids? It is the largest family of plants in the world. Though normally associated with the tropics, they grow in a wide range of habitats, from Alaska to Tierra del Fuego, from sea level to 12,000 feet in the Andes. Sobralias reach 20 feet in height, Grammatophyllums can weigh over a ton and Vanilla, a vining orchid, can reach 400 feet in length, (it is pollinated by a stingless bee). There are tiny orchids of less than a quarter inch and orchids that grow underground and are never seen unless accidentally exposed. In the 1870's and 1880's there was an orchid conservatory at the White House along with buildings for roses, camellias and bedding plants. In 1902 the buildings were demolished to make way for the West wing.

O is the second to last vowel and the fourth most common letter in the English alphabet

OIL:

Did You know that oil, whether animal, mineral or vegetable, and water don't mix, unless emulsified, but did you know why? Oil is immiscible with water. Immiscible means, 'water fearing'. Mineral oils do not come from minerals but from ancient fossilized organic materials, plants and animals.

One 42-gallon barrel of crude oil can produce 19 gallons of gasoline, 10 gals. of diesel, 4 gals. of jet fuel, 2 gals. of heating oil, 3 gals. split between liquefied petroleum, gases and heavy fuel oil (used in ships) and 7 gals. of other products. The total of these various products comes to 45 gallons!

Opera:

Cool fact: In Brussels in 1830 a performance of the Opera "La Muette de Portici," which told the story of a revolt in 17th century Italy, set off a riot. The riot began a revolution that culminated in the founding of the Kingdom of Belgium.

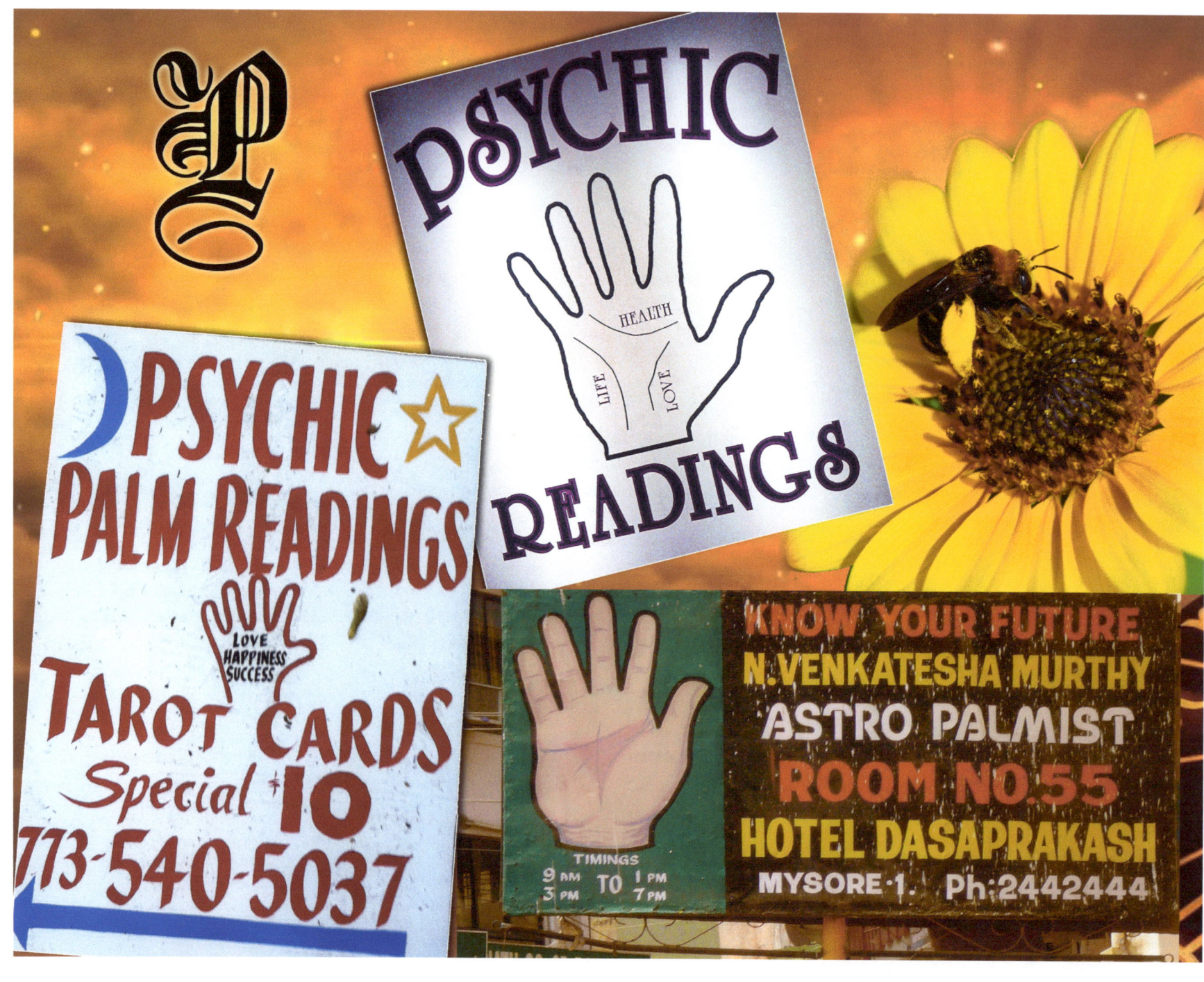

P.

Did you know the longest word in English beginning with P is **Pneumonoultramicroscopicsilicovolcanoconiosis**?

It was made up in 1935 purely to invent a new longest word. Silicosis is still used for the condition the new word was meant to describe.

Palm reading:

Did you know that Palm reading has been around for thousands of years? Where it began no one knows for sure. The Middle and Far East are the main contenders. In just about any town or city in the world you will see a sign for palm reading.

It must be a sustainable business; crossing the reader's palm with silver is the first move to having your palm read. As with any other form of divination there are as many different methods of reading palms as there are ways of interpreting your horoscope. Believe it or not. It's up to you.

Did you know that **pho** is pronounced, FUH?

Proverbs:

Did you know that proverbs are not just grandma's old pithy sayings? The proverbs collected under King Solomon were accumulations of advice, sayings and philosophical thoughts that had been current in the Near East for millennia, meant to guide and govern the way people behaved. It is said that the god of the bible personified wisdom as female and that he acquired wisdom before all else.

Those proverbs that we use today are the thousands of ways people have tried to capture the essence of concepts, values, ideas and perceived wisdom boiled down to easily, and sometimes not so easily, understood quotes. 'A stitch in time saves nine.' 'A bird in the hand is worth two in the bush.'

Such simple, graspable sayings encapsulate concepts of far deeper significance than might appear on the surface. The thinkers and sages of the past strove to communicate their learning to the unschooled in as simple a way as they could. Such proverbs work to this day.

Platitudes:

Platitudes, by comparison, are banal, meaningless statements repeated as if they contained wisdom so obvious as to need no elaboration. Thoughtlessly repeated empty statements that on examination have no real meaning or worth are accepted on face value by those that have unquestioningly bought into concepts and values that only make sense if they are accepted on faith. There are perhaps as many platitudes as there are proverbs and unfortunately, as many, if not more people that live by them.

POLLINATORS:

Did you know that most plants depend upon pollinators in order to fruit and reproduce? Millions of pounds of toxic pesticides are used indiscriminately and are killing off the most important critters on the planet, bees, birds, bats, butterflies, moths and many other insects make life possible for us. We need to protect them.

Q

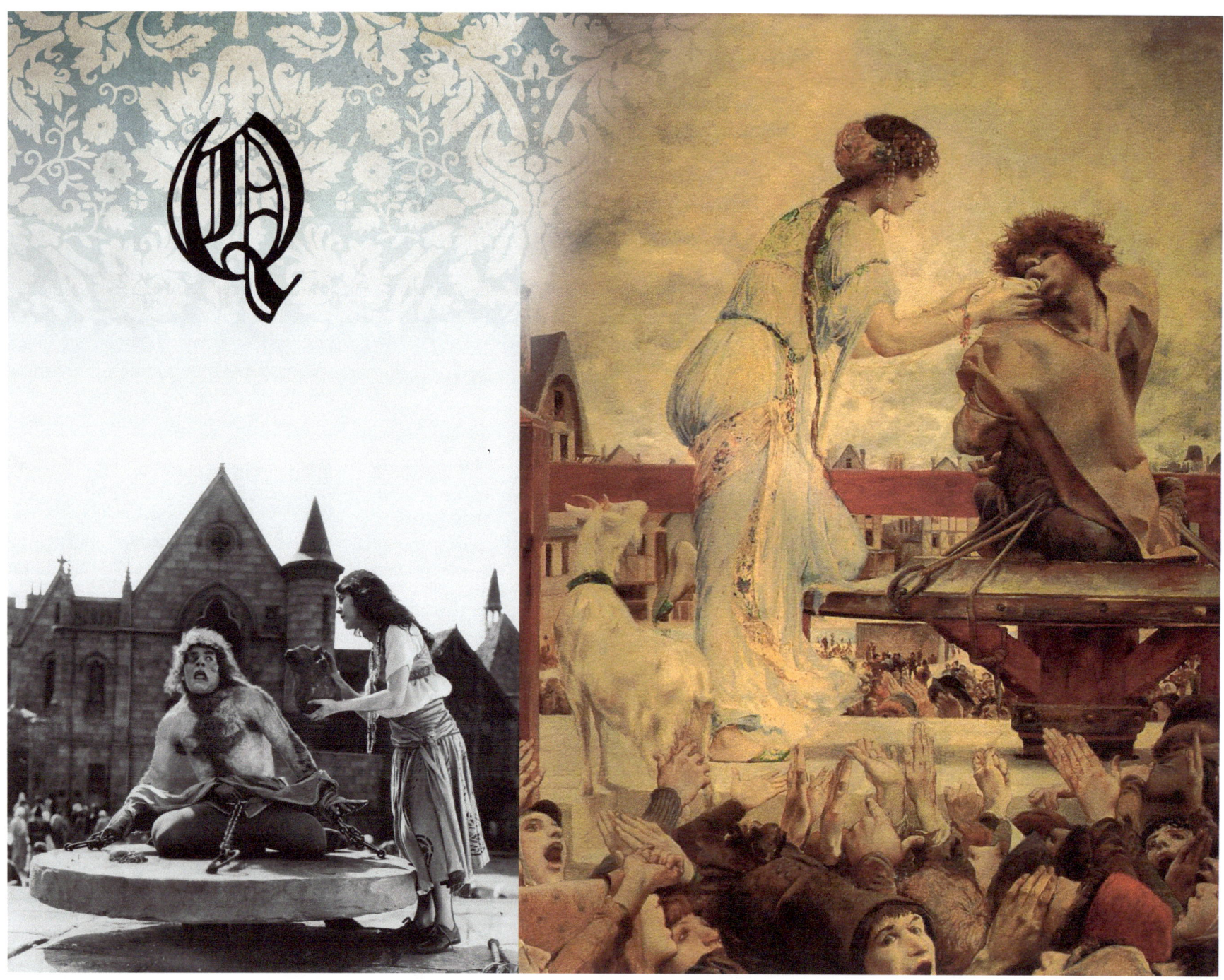

Q.

Quasimodo:

Did you know that Quasimodo, the name of the main protagonist in *The Hunchback of Notre Dame*, comes from *quasi modo geniti infantes,* words spoken on the first Sunday after Easter, the time when the fictional infant hunchback was abandoned at the cathedral?

Victor Hugo entitled his book, *Notre-Dame de Paris* as it was intended to alert the people of Paris to the fact that Gothic architecture, of which Notre Dame was a splendid example, was being neglected, destroyed and defaced by the addition of new 'improvements.' The English translator changed the title to, *The Hunchback of Notre Dame*. The love that the deaf, deformed bell-ringer forms for the gypsy Esmeralda struck a nerve which has resulted in a number of film versions, TV and radio versions, plays, musicals, an opera, ballets, music compositions and a video game.

Queen:

The word queen comes from Middle English *quene* and Old English *cwēn* meaning woman, wife. Then, King's wife. In Hebrew shegal means King's wife. Malkah, meaning one actually reigning as a queen, does not appear in the Bible until mention of the Queen of Sheba. The name has been applied to fertile females of various species — ants, bees, termites and queen naked-mole-rats.

Females that are elected or chosen, by popular acclaim or by judges, are named queen: Beauty Queen, Movie Queen, May Queen or Queen of Heaven. Cleopatra was known as the Queen of the Nile. Campy or effeminate male homosexuals are often referred to as queens, drag queens or queen bees. Queen is used as a given name. I had an auntie Queen, my mother's sister. Queen Latifa is a well-known American actress.

Quinoa:

Did you know that quinoa is pronounced KEEN-wah? Full of fiber, high in protein, iron, magnesium, manganese, essential amino acids and gluten-free, quinoa is a species of goosefoot (*Chenopodium quinoa**). It's related to beetroot and amaranth. It is native to the Andes Mountains in Bolivia, Chile and Peru where wild varieties were used for centuries before it was domesticated 3000-4000 years ago.

The seed coating must be removed before eating as it contains bitter saponin. This bitterness keeps birds from eating it. The saponin is used in detergents. The leaves are also edible. Quinoa is a Quechua word. The Inca, who spoke Quechua, held Quinoa as sacred. Because it was used in their religious ceremonies, the Spanish conquistadors forbade its cultivation, forcing the Inca to grow wheat instead. Now popular again, quinoa is under cultivation in many different parts of the world.

Cool fact: Jews, using quinoa as a substitute for leavened grains, which are forbidden during Passover, were told by some certification boards that for various reasons, one being that it resembled prohibited grains, quinoa was not Kosher. In 2013 The Orthodox Union, the world's largest Kosher certification agency, announced it would certify quinoa as Kosher.

*Lamb's quarters is also in the Goosefoot family. For information and a painting of Lamb's quarters see my, *"A to Z book of Weeds and other Useful Plants."* (Published by Strategic book publishing and Rights agency) A second edition will soon be published by, Erin Go Bragh Publishing.

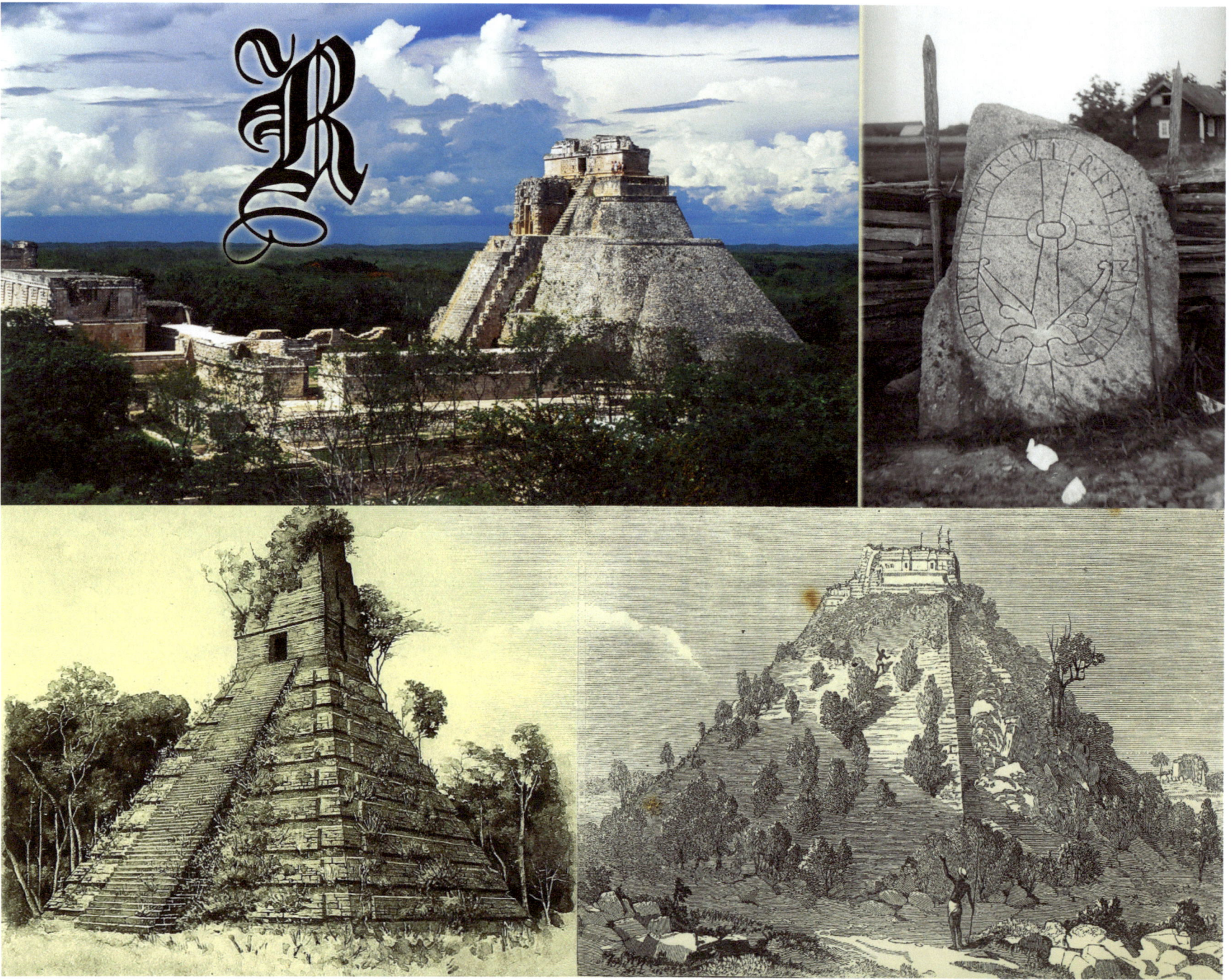

R.

Ruins:

Did you know the Maya ruins at Palenque, Chiapas, Mexico. are still being explored? Newly found artifacts attest to the exceptional beauty of the architecture and art of the people that once lived there. Recently more unknown Maya sites were discovered in Guatemala. All over the world the ruins of past civilizations are still showing up. Whether destroyed by natural disasters, leveled by invaders, simply abandoned or buried by the inhabitants when they moved on, washed away by floods, inundated by the sea or lost to the jungle, ruins fascinate more than archaeologists and anthropologists, but it is they who make it possible for us to know something of the lives of those that built and inhabited these long-lost places.

Did you know that the remains of a city beside the Macon River in northeastern Louisiana called Poverty Point are as old as the pyramids of Egypt? A 72' high mound consisting of 8 million cubic feet of earth stands behind six semi-circular ridges three quarters of a mile across, all built by hunter/gatherers who moved the earth one basket full at a time. The city was part of a wide trade network. Archaeologists have found stones and copper imported from thousands of miles away. On the ridges where the people lived, pottery, figurines, artifacts, projectile points and the remains of fire hearths have been found. The city thrived for 600 years. Why it was abandoned is yet to be discovered.

Did you know in 2014 archaeologists found the remains of an ancient village of 75 structures in Arizona's Petrified Forest National Park? During a two-year period, it was the second village of such size to be found.

Runes:

The oldest known inscription in the runic alphabet dates from around 150CE. Though its source of origin is unknown, it is thought to have been used first by Germanic people, though there are Scandinavian versions and it even made its way into England. Used for centuries, it eventually lost out to Gothic and Latin alphabets. Like other alphabets it was alleged to be a gift from god, in this case, the god Odin, thus it had to have magical properties and could be used for divination.

Though it wouldn't be surprising, there is little evidence showing the runes were actually used for such purposes; this has not stopped modern authors, most notably, Ralph Blum, from devising methods of using the runes as systems of fortune telling similar to Tarot cards or yarrow sticks.

Rhea:

Did you know that in ancient Greek religion the goddess Rhea, the mother of Zeus, tricked her husband Cronus into swallowing a stone he thought was actually his new born son? (He was convinced that any child of his would overthrow him just as he had his father.) Rhea gave the child to Almathea, the goddess of nourishment, to raise. Almathea could turn herself into a goat and when one of her horns fell off she filled it with herbs, fruit and other goodies.

Zeus gave the horn the magical power to fill with whatever one wished to receive. Hence, we have cornucopia, from the Latin, *cornu copiae*, horn of plenty. There's an old saying, 'The Greeks had a word for it.' Why Latin is used in this case, I don't know.

Common adverse effects of Tobacco smoking

- Larynx cancer
- Oral cavity cancer
- Esophagus cancer
- **Myocardial infarction**
- **Lung cancer**
- **Chronic bronchitis**
- **Emphysema**
- **Systemic atherosclerosis**
- Peptic ulcer
- Bladder cancer
- Pancreas cancer

S. Did you know the longest word in English beginning with S is **Supercalifragilisticexpialidocious**?

A made-up song title for the film "Mary Poppins". The brothers who wrote the song said they heard it as kids. A woman claimed she invented it, with a slightly different spelling in 1931, and a pair of songwriters claimed that they invented it in 1947. It is in the Oxford English Dictionary.

Sleep:

Did you know medical studies show that taking less than 6 to 8 hours of sleep a night or experiencing interrupted sleep has many bad health effects? Children require even more and the younger they are the more they need. Even working night shifts, studies have shown, result in serious, though possibly temporary, mental health problems. Conditions such as insomnia, apnea and other sleep disorders can often be cured by changes in one's diet, exercise routine or living habits more effectively than resorting to drugs.

Sleep aids, both over the counter and prescription, account for a large part of the pharmaceutical industry's income. Yet in the past and in some societies today, the "go to bed and sleep 6-8 hours" pattern is not the norm. Without the 8am to 5pm work schedule people can sleep when they feel like it. Nomads, hunter/gatherers and extended family groups who live in close quarters tend to sleep and wake for short periods throughout the day and night, depending on what is happening within the group. This kind of fragmented sleep should result in a risk of depression, bipolar disorder, type2 diabetes and impaired memory. Though this doesn't appear to be the case.

Cool fact: Dolphins, whales and seals have what is known as 'unihemispheric' sleep, which allows one brain hemisphere to sleep while the other remains fully functional. The hemispheres alternate during the sleep period so that each gets sufficient rest. This way they avoid suffocating or drowning and it keeps them from becoming easy prey to predators. Adult dolphins and whales can go without sleep for a month. Albatrosses and some other birds stay aloft for long periods of time employing the same sleep technique.

Spleen:

Did you know the spleen is the largest organ in the lymphatic system? It keeps bodily fluids balanced and fights infection. If the spleen is removed, the liver and other lymph nodes take up its duties. However, there is a greater risk of getting infections. If you get in a rage and start shouting you are "venting your spleen".

Smoking:

In recent years we have learned more about the ill effects of Smoking, but did you know that in the seventeenth century, shortly after Sir Walter Raleigh introduced tobacco to the old world from America, King James of England called it "a custome loathsome to the eye, hateful to the nose, harmful to the brain and dangerous to the lungs"? A few years later, the Ming emperor, Ch'ung Chen of China ruled that anyone importing or using tobacco would have their head cut off!

Shroud of Turin:

The Shroud of Turin is a piece of cloth believed by many to have wrapped the body of Jesus of Nazareth after he was crucified. It bears the imprint of a body that so far has defied all efforts to determine how it was applied. Some tests show the bloodstains to be paint, others confer blood, carbon-dating has indicated that the cloth was woven in the 13th century, but this also is contested. The Roman Catholic Church does not claim that the cloth is authentic but it is periodically displayed and millions of people go to look at it.

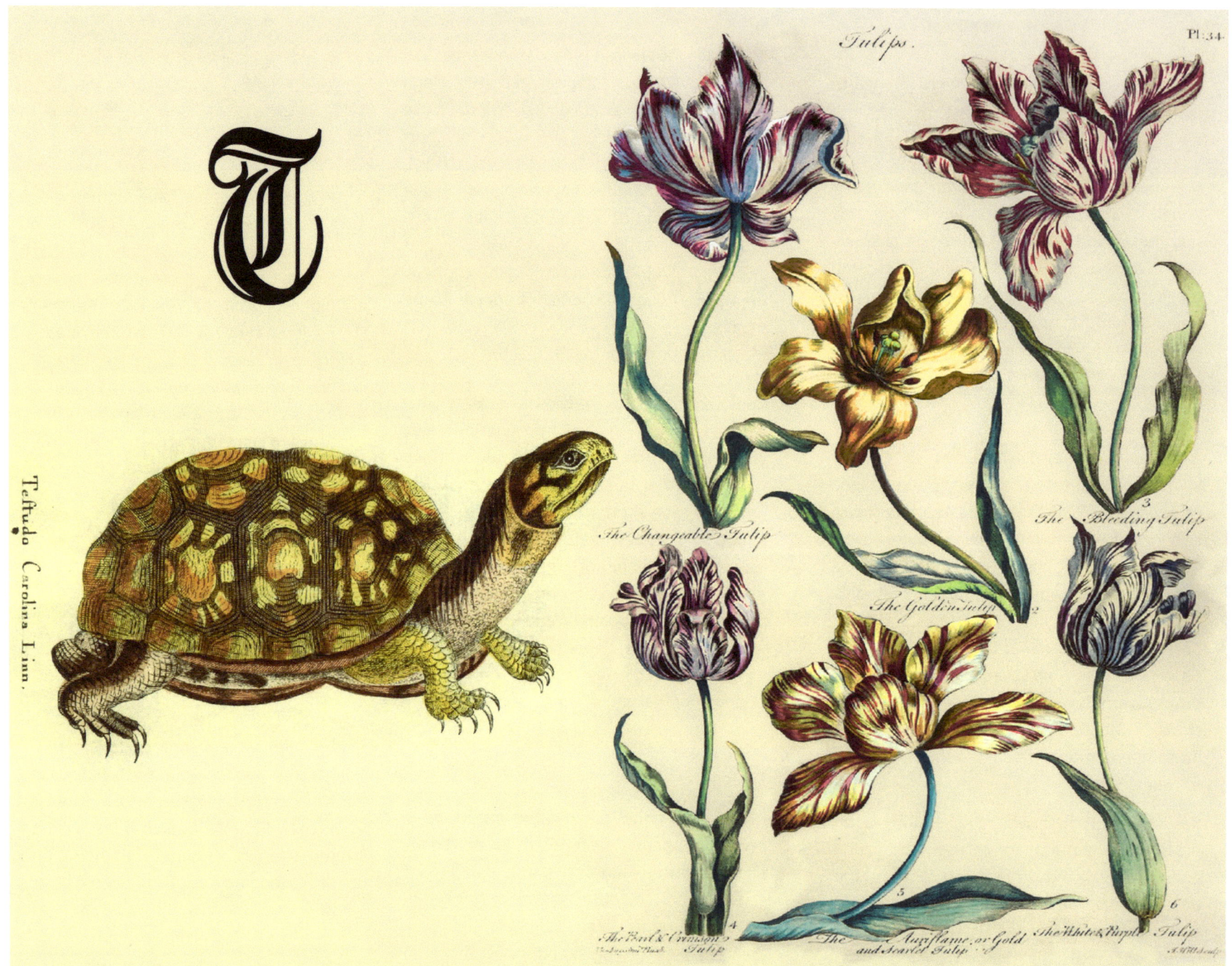

T. Did you know that turmeric, a plant with many health benefits used in cooking, is pronounced, TUR-mer-ik?

Did you know that **Tlingit**, the name of the Native Americans who live in southeastern Alaska, is pronounced, kling-KIT?

Tarantella :

Did you know that a number of theories have been proposed for the origins of the dance called the Tarantella? One proposal is that the cult of Dionysis, in which usually drug induced, frenzied, dancing took place, so alarmed the Roman Senate that the cult was outlawed. Driven underground, it surfaced as a cure for spider bite victims! This "therapy" that required dancing for hours or even days on end to sweat it out, so to speak, was called the tarantella for the tarantula wolf spider, *Lycosa tarantula,* that was suspected of inflicting the bite that sickened people, although it is more likely to have been the highly venomous Mediterranean black widow.

The tarantella became a popular dance performed to fast, cheerful music played on the mandolin, accordion and tambourine. It is believed to have originated in the town of Taranto and like the tarantula wolf spider, was named for the town. Ironically, the *Lycosa tarantula* is a different species and not actually related to the tarantula, a spider not dangerous to humans and one that is a popular pet. So, don't step on that tarantula!

Cool fact: In the Disney film "Cinderella," the fairy godmother's song *Bibbidi-Bobbidi-Boo* is a tarantella. Many classical composers including, Chopin, Liszt, Mendelssohn, Debussy, Prokofiev and Stravinsky included a tarantella in their works.

Testify:

Did you know that in Roman days when men swore they were telling the truth, they grasped their testicles with their right hand. From this custom comes the word 'testify'.

Turtles, Tortoises & Terrapins:

Did you know turtles, tortoises and terrapins are all members of the chelonian family? The land dwellers are commonly called tortoises, the water dwellers, turtles. Terrapin is an Algonquian Indian word for the turtles that live in brackish water. Turtles have webbed feet, tortoises have clawed feet and the amphibious turtles have webbed feet with claws.

In the summer, sea turtles hit the beach in their thousands to nest (kind of like college students). Each female lays about a hundred eggs in the sand. Though many of these nesting beaches are protected, eggs are still dug up for eating by people and animals. Remaining eggs hatch out some two months later when the hatchlings dig their way out and head for the water. Predators on land, from the air and in the water see to it that only 2% survive. Some 173,000 turtles were killed by the 2010 BP oil spill in the Gulf of Mexico. As of 2017 sea creatures, birds and cleanup workers continue to suffer from the effects of the spill.

Tulip:

Did you know that the Tulip craze that hit Holland in 1632 grew to the point where farms and whole estates were traded for a few bulbs? The tulip was introduced to Holland in the early 17th century from Asia Minor. By 1634 all kinds of people were growing bulbs which were sold before they bloomed. Contracts were bought and sold several times before they were delivered and the prices skyrocketed. More specimens were being created as the wealthy tried to outdo each other with the uniqueness of their collections. In 1637 the market in Tulips crashed, partly due to forces having nothing to do with the business but the government did decide to step in and the 'tulip mania' bubble burst.

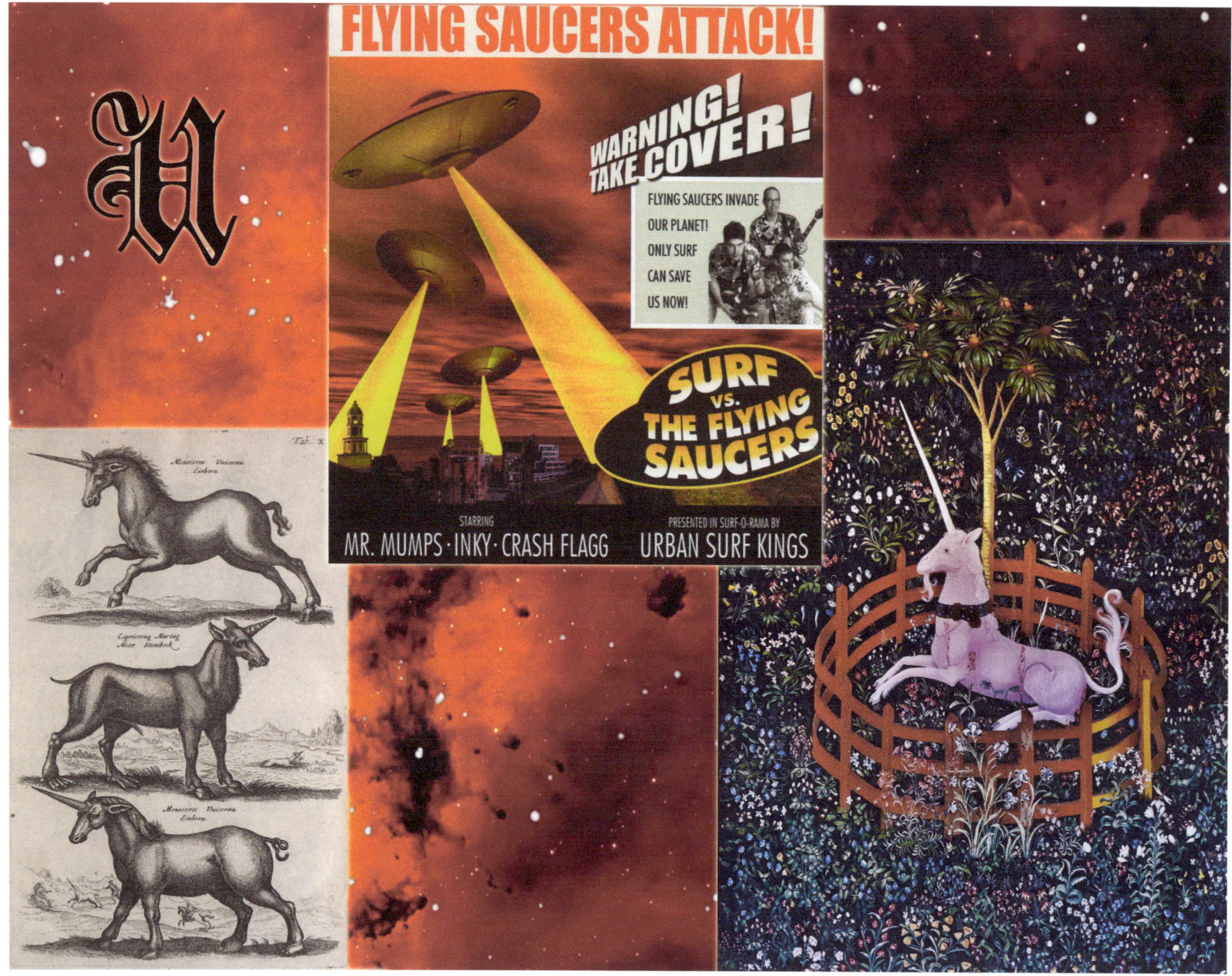

U.

UFO:

Did you know that even before the size of the visible universe was known, the idea that life might exist outside of our planet was around and records of UFO sightings have been found dating back many centuries? Alien objects in the sky, unexplained lights moving erratically, reports of alien abductions, landings and crashes, films and photos of UFOs and their extraterrestrial passengers, offer persuasive evidence for the existence of intelligent life forms having visited our planet.

Unfortunately, despite the seeming abundance of material on the subject, it is still not possible, given the poor quality and the alternative interpretations of the images presented, the unreliability of oral testimony, the hoaxes, government denials and misreporting available to us, to say there is conclusive evidence that such reports are true. There are many, many convinced people who will cite the Roswell, NM. crash of 1947, the Aurora, TX. crash of 1897, crop circles and the myriad eyewitness reports, some of which date back thousands of years, as irrefutable evidence.

As with so many things begging explanation, the jury is still out and whatever conclusions are drawn, there will always be those who disagree with the verdict, that is until there are lots of little green men walking around.

Unicorns:

Unicorns are mostly depicted as a pretty horse, sometimes with cloven hoofs and a swirling horn on its forehead. The Roman naturalist Pliny the elder, A.D.23- A.D.79, described it this way: "A very ferocious beast, with the body of a horse, the head of a deer, the feet of an elephant, the tail of a boar, a deep bellowing voice and a black horn, two cubits (35feet) long."

In spite of a complete lack of evidence for any such creature, the Unicorn managed to make its way into Christian myths and into heraldry. The Royal arms of the United Kingdom has a lion, representing England and a unicorn, representing Scotland. Books, toys and films abound with stories of its nature and behavior. All of it the product of the imagination. Rhinoceroses have been called, obese unicorns.

University:

Did you know that the first University was founded in India early in the fifth century CE? It was another six hundred years before the first European university was established. The Nalanda University eventually had ten thousand students from all over Asia. Aside from giving instruction in the arts and sciences, Buddhist religion and philosophy were taught. Predictably, in the twelfth century invading armies from outside India killed all the teachers, razed the campus and demolished all the statues of Buddha.

Utopia:

Cool fact: Utopia, we think of as denoting an idyllic, paradisical or Eden-like place. The word was coined by Sir Thomas More based on a Greek word meaning 'no-place' or a non-existent place that was better than the one the reader happened to be in. Not exactly what we would call Utopia.

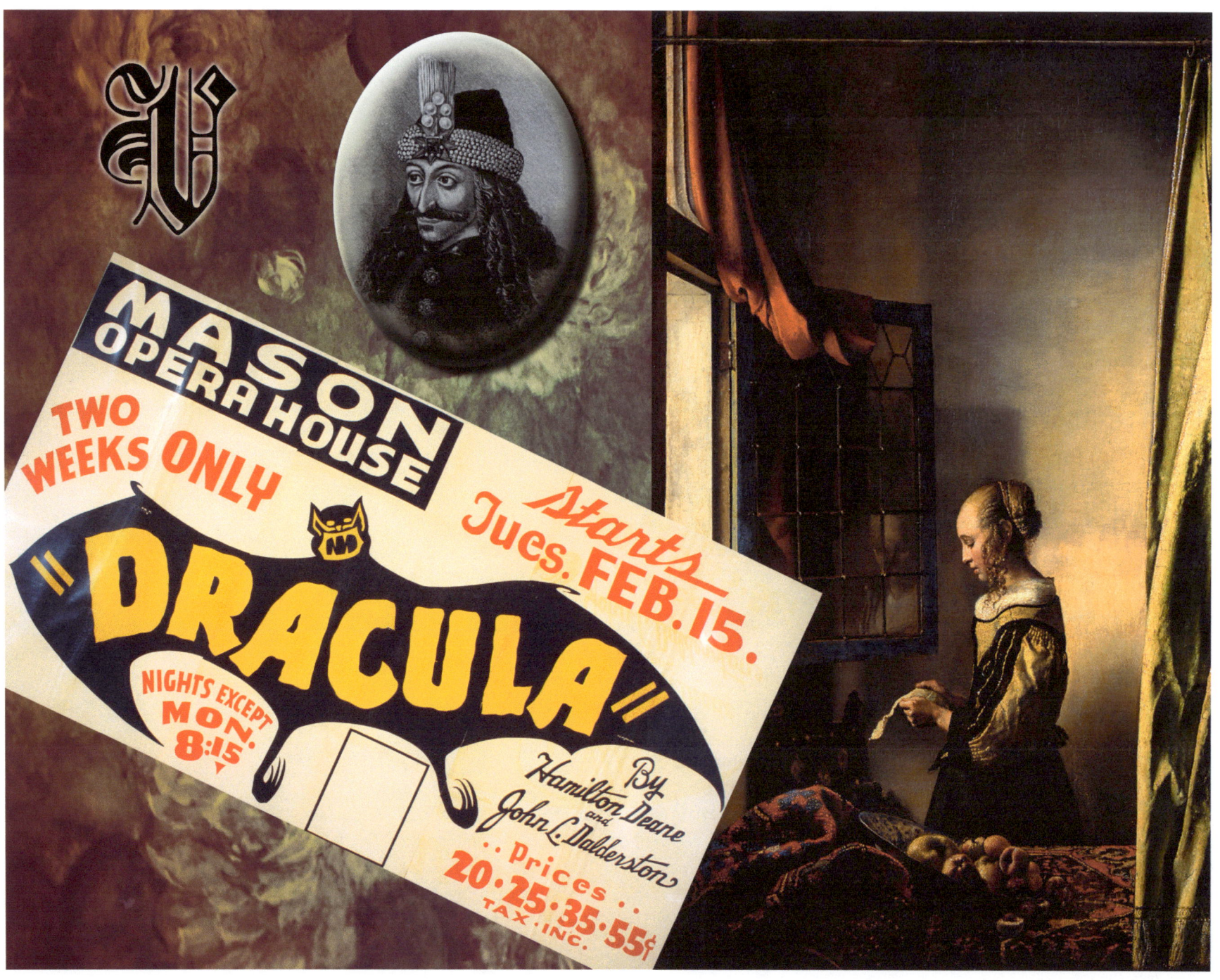

V.

Vampires

Prince Vlad Tepes (1431-1476) of Romania is said to be the model for Bram Stoker's Dracula, perhaps the most famous vampire. However, in Romania the prince is a national hero for defending his empire from the Ottoman Turks.

So many myths and legends exist around the world of "undead" blood drinking beings that it is virtually impossible not to believe that there is some truth to the stories. Whether observation of creatures such as leeches, lampreys or vampire bats that do drain blood from other animals for sustenance, gave rise to the idea or whether attempts to come to terms with death, what death is and what comes after, lead to such imaginative conjectures, is hard to know. It is clear, however, from the seemingly never-ending stream of books, movies and television shows about vampires, that speculation about death and whether it is possible to avoid it still has a powerful attraction for many humans.

Cool fact: Because blood is so rich in iron anyone consuming it on a regular basis would get very sick. *Haemochromatosis* (iron overdose) causes a wide range of health problems including liver and nervous system damage.

Vermeer:

Did you know that during WWII the Nazis looted innumerable art objects, intended for a museum Adolf Hitler planned to build? Among the 6,750 works of art found hidden by the Nazis in an Austrian salt mine were two paintings by the Dutch painter Jan Vermeer (1632-1675). One was a previously unknown Vermeer.

This painting, *The Adulterous Woman*, caused a stir in the art world as so few Vermeer's were known to exist. Among the Nazi haul was found a receipt for the painting which showed that Herman Goering, the Nazi propaganda minster, bought the painting from art dealer Alois Miedl acting on behalf of Han van Meegeren, a once popular Dutch artist. Meegeren was charged with collaborating with the enemy, which carried the death sentence, and for illegally selling a national treasure. Under interrogation van Meegeren finally confessed that the painting was a fake that he himself had painted!

He also claimed to have painted all the other 'new' Vermeer's that had appeared in recent years, paintings that had been authenticated by eminent scholars and art professors. This caused a sensation such that in order to prove his claims, van Meegeren painted a 'Vermeer' in his prison cell whilst describing the techniques he used to make the paintings look as though they were painted centuries earlier. Naturally, he was acquitted. Van Meegeren went on to produce more paintings that were so sought after that others began to paint fake van Meegeren's!

Cool fact: Nothing is known about Vermeer's childhood. It is not known how he decided to become a painter or where he trained. In order to be admitted to the guild of Saint Luke, the powerful trade association for artists, an apprenticeship was required, a masterwork presented, plus a fee was to be paid. Whether or not Vermeer followed this procedure, he was admitted to the guild in 1653.

Vermeer was not particularly successful. He died leaving his wife and children in debt, and wouldn't you know, Van Meegeren died a millionaire. It was not until the 19th century that Vermeer began to achieve fame and is now the Dutch painter ranked alongside Rembrandt and Frans Hals. It has been posited that Vermeer used a camera oscura or some other type of optic device to achieve the almost photo realistic detail in his work. True or not, it takes nothing away from the greatness of his work.

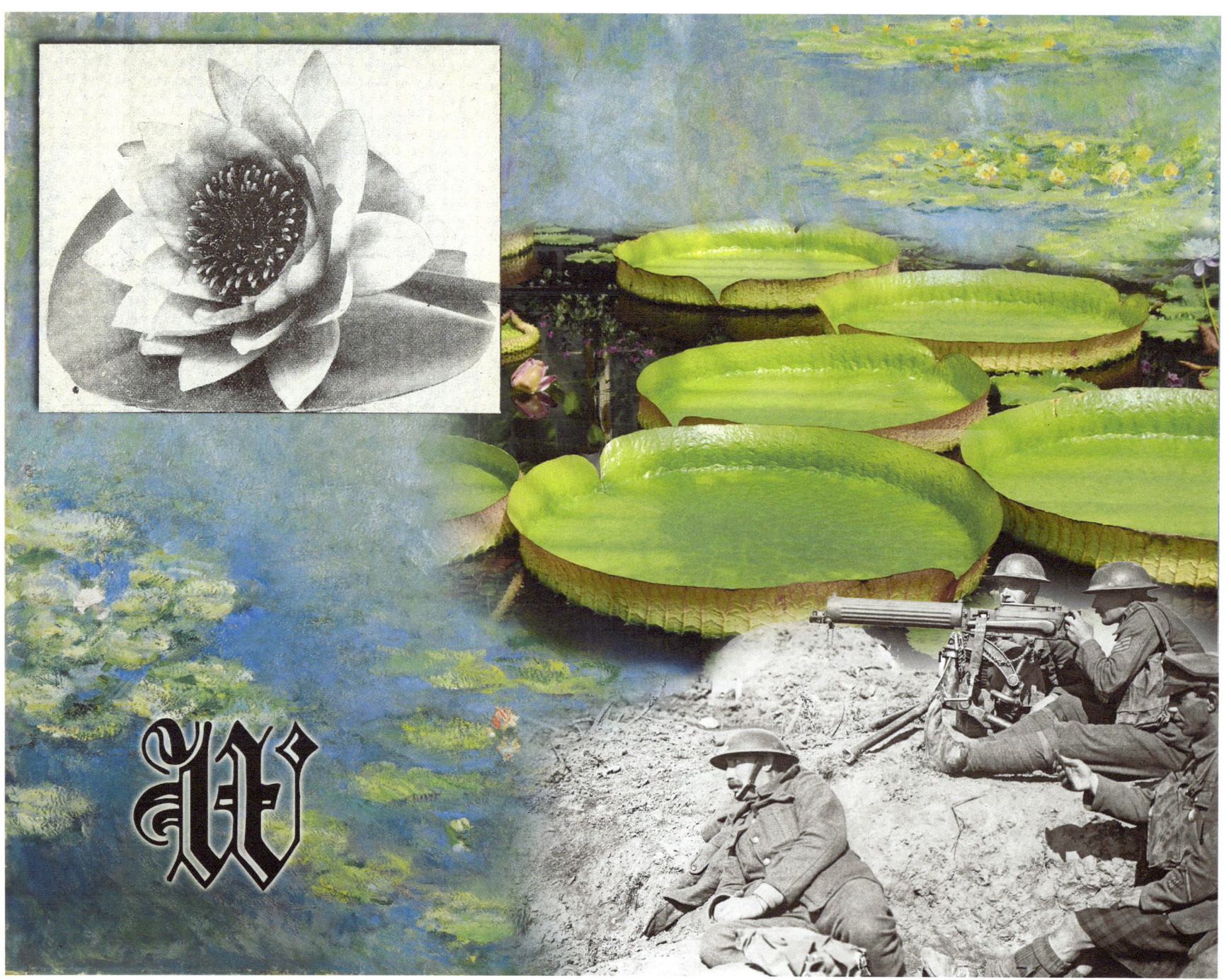

W. Did you know that the silent **W** of **wr** words were once pronounced in Anglo-Saxon?

Of ancient German origin, such words as; 'gnaw', 'wreck', 'knack', etc. were also pronounced as written. 'Loaf,' 'rough' and 'neck' would be written as 'hloaf,' 'hrough' and 'hneck' today, if the silent h hadn't been dropped in English sometime around the 13th Century. 'When' and 'white' were written as 'hwen' and hwite' back then. We just haven't gotten around to dropping the silent W, yet. The K of know, knight, knock, etc. became silent around the 16th to 17th centuries. Why? Or hwy? You might ask.

Water lilies:

Did you know that the giant water lily or Vitória Régina is one of the largest aquatic plants in the world? The leaves, or pads, reach 2.5 m. in diameter. In an origin story of the Tupi-Guarani people of Brazil the moon was believed to be the goddess Jaci who, at night, when she went down behind the mountains, would take the beautiful virgins of the village with her and turn them into stars. Naiá, one of the village virgins, desperate to become a star, seeing the moon's reflection in a lake, dove in and was drowned. For this sacrifice, the goddess turned the girl into a different star, "the star of the waters," the giant water lily.

Water lilies by Claude Monet (1840-1926) are a series of about 250 oil paintings from his flower garden in Giverny, France. They were the main focus of his work for the last 30 years of his life. Many were completed while he suffered from cataracts. In June 2007 one of these water lily paintings sold for $18.5 million. In 2008 another sold for $41 million.

Water:

Did you know that can you drink too much water? Drinking a lot of water in a short space of time can result in many health problems and even death. Water poisoning, water intoxication, occurs when the amount of water in the blood exceeds the amount the body can excrete. The electrolytes in your blood become diluted and sodium levels drop. Once they drop below a certain level you have hynonatremia, a potentially life-threatening condition. Drink less than a half-gallon per hour or stick to the often recommended 8, 8oz. glasses per day or drink when you feel thirsty unless you are sweating excessively due to work or play. Older adults and pregnant women may need a little more. Don't drink too much, don't drink too little.

War:

Did you know that War and its aftermath may have killed more people than any disease, epidemic, famine or other disasters; displaced more people; injured, maimed and produced more mental and other long term medical problems; resulted in the loss of countless cultural treasures and destroyed more property than any other human endeavor? In WWII the USSR had 13,600,000 military losses, Germany, 10,000,000. The millions of civilian dead we are not counting (okay, 26,600,000 in the USSR alone). Wars continue with more of the same. Yet for some unknown reason, being in the military is considered a good and noble thing. Anybody that has been in the military knows that stupifying waste is the rule. Most countries have standing armies which essentially amounts to welfare. Aside from the enormous cost in equipment, there is the housing, clothing, and feeding of personnel and the equivalent of a socialized medical service, which continues for the rest of their lives. Since it is mostly the young and naïve who are recruited into the military, is it possible an education that addresses the question of war differently, might someday produce human beings that would not order others to kill people and people who would refuse to obey such orders?

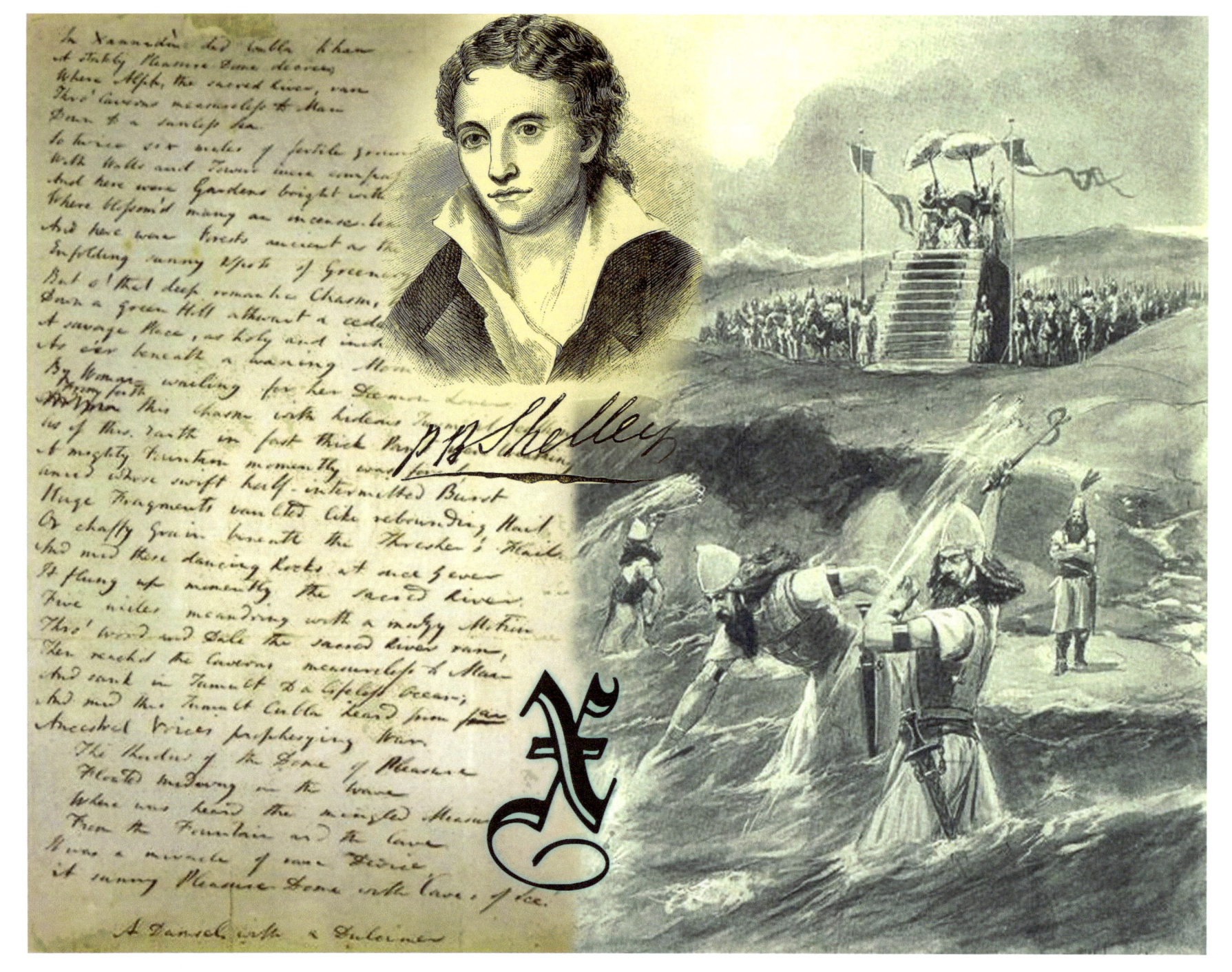

X. Xanadu is pronounced za-na-du

We mostly know the word Xanadu from the opening line of the Samuel Taylor Coleridge poem "Kubla Khan"

"In Xanadu did Kubla Khan a stately pleasure dome decree" Or as the name of the house that Charles Foster Kane builds in California in the film "Citizen Kane."

Did you know that Xanadu is a modification of Xandu, the modern Shangtu, site of Kubla Khan's summer residence in China? In 1260 it was there that Kubla, grandson of Genghis Khan, held an assembly and had himself elected Khan.

The Mongols under Genghis Khan had conquered large areas of Russia, Persia, Mongolia and China. Kubla Khan completed the conquest of China, establishing a united nation that had been divided since the Tang Dynasty, (618-907).

Marco Polo's description of Kubla Khan's Xanadu, which he may have visited in 1275, appeared in a book that Coleridge was reading just before falling into an opium-induced sleep during which he dreamed 200-300 lines of his poem, "Kubla Khan". Awakening, Coleridge managed to jot down some of the words that he vividly remembered.

Unfortunately, he was interrupted before he could write down the whole poem and when he returned to it was unable to recall the rest. The poem remains a fragment of only 54 lines.

Cool Fact: Although paper money had been used in China before, under Kubla Khan it became the sole medium of exchange.

Xenophobia :

Did you know Xenophobia is the abnormal fear of the politics or culture of foreigners or that which is considered strange or unfamiliar? Xenophobia reaches its peak at time of war or during the migration of people from one country to another, one often being the result of the other. Prejudice, racism and usually violence are the result.

Xerxes:

Xerxes I of Persia (519 BCE-465 BCE) built two pontoon bridges across the strait of Hellespont to facilitate his invasion of Greece. When the bridges were destroyed by a storm, Xerxes had the strait whipped 300 times and had chains placed on the water (that'll teach 'em a lesson!). His second attempt to cross was successful and the battle of Thermopylae followed. Having defeated the Greeks, Xerxes burnt Athens to the ground.

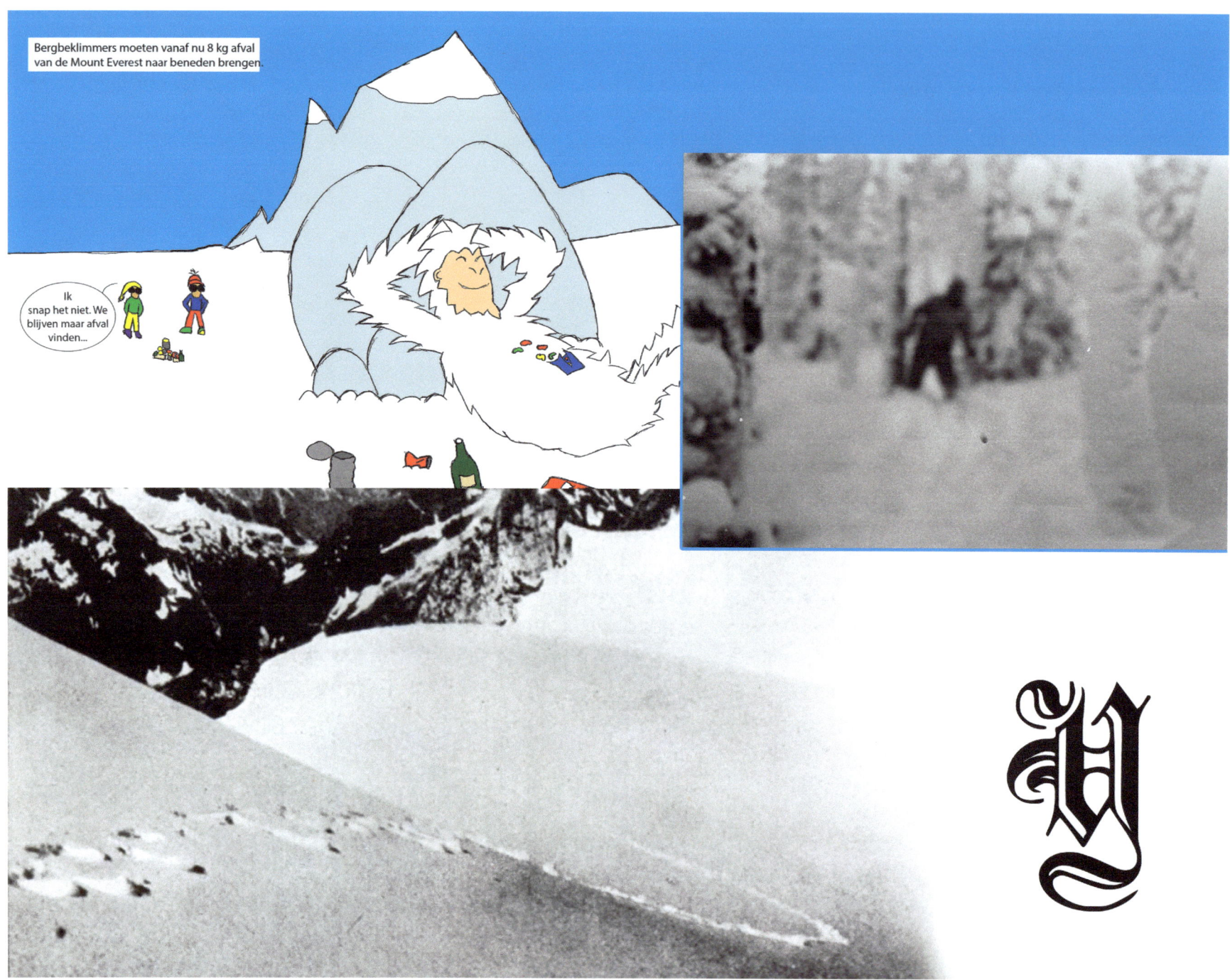

Y.

Yeti:

Did you know that there are records of sightings of the Yeti dating back to the 6th century BCE? The Yeti, or abominable snowman as it is often called, is reputed to inhabit remote glaciers in the Himalayas that cover parts of Tibet, Nepal, India and Pakistan. Like the American Sasquatch or Bigfoot, there are many stories of encounters, footprints, fur and bones all purportedly proving the existence of such a creature. None have stood up to scrutiny. Expeditions have been mounted, tests have been carried out, yet no irrefutable evidence has yet appeared as to the Yeti's existence. Theories and opinions abound, as they always will. One must always remember that the existence of the Gorilla and the Panda were once doubted and new species are still being discovered. As with ETs, no conclusive evidence of their existence has been presented to the world or at least none that is generally accepted by scientists or the public at large.

Translation for the Yeti cartoon:

Mountaineer, from now on we need to take 8kg. of waste down from Mount Everest. "I don't get it. We keep finding waste." Note: Yetis are *not* creating the waste.

Yule log:

Did you know that burning the Yule log was a practice adopted by Christianity from pagans? Like many pre-Christian activities that resisted suppression, the Yule log was co-opted by the church and attached to Christmas, which for symbolic reasons was enacted at the time of the winter solstice. In northern countries, on the shortest day of the year, the Yule log was burned to encourage the sun to return and for the days to lengthen again. This sense of hope and renewal was attached to the birth of the Christ, conveniently set at December 25th, making the Yule log a useful metaphor.

Yeast:

Did you know that yeast is a fungus just like mushrooms, the molds in ripe cheese and the molds used in medicine as antibiotics? In baking, dough rises because the added yeast, in the process of digesting sugars in the flour, produces carbon dioxide gas that inflates the stretchy and elastic dough. Usually, after the first rising the dough is punched down and then allowed to rise again. Loaf size pieces are then kneaded, allowed to rise once more before being placed in the oven to bake. Even though there are 1500 species of yeast, it is estimated that they constitute only 1% of all described fungal species. The ancient Egyptians used yeast in baking and beer making. It wasn't until the 18th century that a technique to remove the liquid from yeast allowed for the production of solid blocks of yeast which later led to the availability of granulated yeast. Nutritional yeasts are excellent sources of protein and vitamins while pathogenic yeasts cause infections that lead to hundreds of thousands of deaths annually.

Huitlacoche (Weet- la-coach-ay) may not be a yeast but it is a fungus that grows on young maize. It has been a popular and highly nutritious food ever since the Aztecs made use of it and thereafter intentionally inoculated corn with the spores in order to produce more of what is in fact a disease, one highly sought after by discerning gourmets.

Cool fact: Very ripe berries are of great attraction to birds in the fall. Yeast organisms ferment the fruit, making it alcoholic.

Yours or **Yours truly** and its variations as a sign off has been used in letter writing for centuries. "Yours, etc." appeared in Jane Austen's "Pride and Prejudice." This leaves open all kinds of fun possibilities. I am sure you can think of some. Yours respectfully, the author.

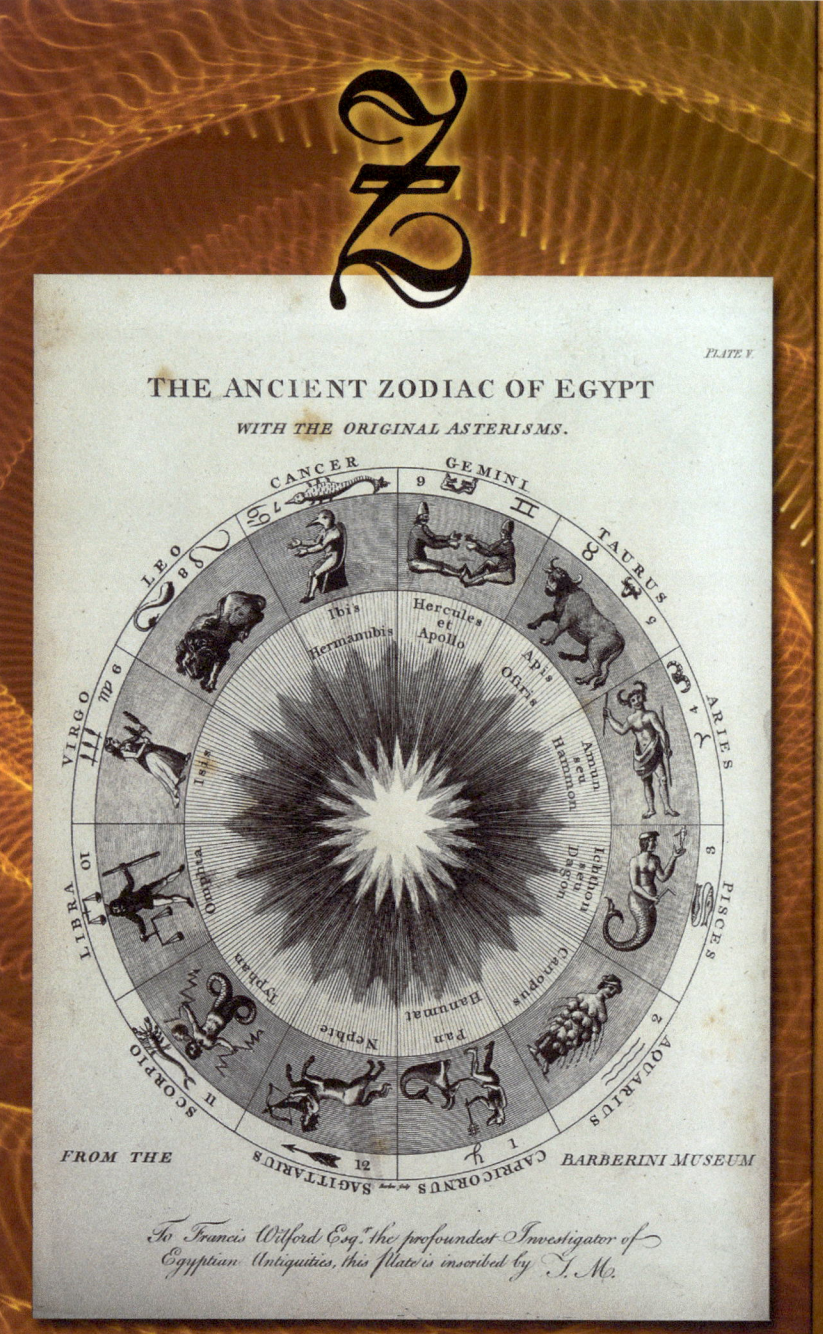

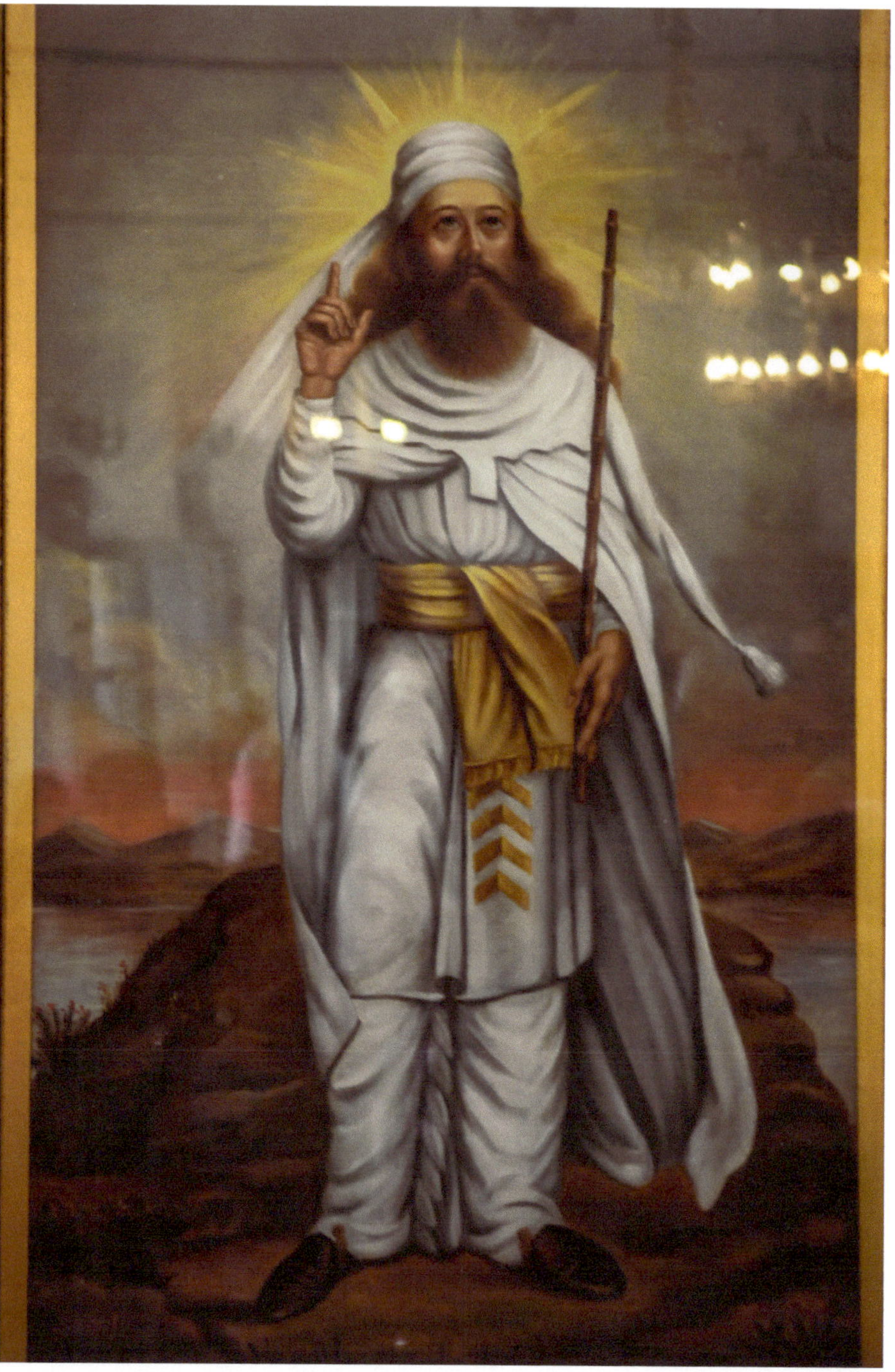

Z is for **Zarathustra**

Did you know that the Richard Strauss (1864-1949) tone poem "Also Sprach Zarathustra," perhaps best known for its use in the opening sequence of Stanley Kubrick's 1968 film "2001, A Space Odyssey," was inspired by the philosophical novel, *"Thus spake Zarathustra"* by Friedrich Nietzsche (1844-1900)?

Zarathustra or Zoroaster was the founder of Zoroastrianism, the official religion of the Sassanid Empire of Persia from 600BCE to 650BCE. It is still practiced today, primarily by the Parsi of India. Very little is known about Zarathustra — where he was born, where he lived or who he was. Scholars differ wildly over when he lived, ranging from 10,000 BCE to the 6th century BCE.

After the god Ahuramazda appeared to him he began to preach. Opposed by the established religions of the time he managed to make converts and his teachings, which influenced the Greeks, Judaism, Islam and Christianity, prevailed.

As with all religions, what its founder might have thought, said or taught passed through the interpretation, re-interpretation and pure invention of those that came after him. Additionally, much of what was known about Zarathustra was lost when successive invaders burned records and libraries. Arab Muslims also killed anyone who refused to adopt Islam.

We do know that the basic tenets of Zoroastrianism are,- good thoughts, good words, good deeds.

Cool fact: Zarathustra is apparently still making public addresses as he has for the last six decades, through various 'Messengers.'

Zero:

Did you know that the Maya invented ZERO centuries before the Hindus? Using just three symbols, the conch sea shell for zero, a dot for one and a bar for five, they were able to make calculations of enormous amounts.

With this vestigial system and their knowledge of astronomy the Maya could accurately date when events had happened long ago in the past and foretell when they would happen in the future.

Zodiac:

Did you know that the twelve houses of the Zodiac were named by Sumerian astronomers to represent the constellations that divide the year into twelve months?

It has been concluded that these divisions were known before the Sumerian era and that the length of the precessional cycle was known (the 2,160 years of one zodiacal house before the shift to the next).

This astronomical knowledge quickly became linked to astrology as certain times appeared to be lucky or unlucky and as the changing seasons brought their attendant pleasures or woes. The symbols associated with each house in the zodiac and the order in which they appear have remained virtually unchanged for six thousand years or more.

Bibliography:

Chatwin, Bruce. 1998. *What Am I Doing Here*. Vintage Publishing

Bryson, Bill. 1990. *The Lost Continent*. HarperCollins Books

Carson, Ciaran. 1999. *Fishing for Amber*. Granta Books

Shlain, Leonard. 1998. *The Alphabet Versus The Goddess*. Compass, Penguin Books

Wulf, Andre. 2016. *The Invention of Nature: Alexander von Humboldt's New World*. Knopf

Sitchin, Zecharia. 1993. *When Time Began*. Avon Books

Torres, Javier Covo. 2007. *The Mayas on the Rocks*. Dante

The New Yorker Magazine   Advanced Magazine Publishers Inc.

Wikipedia

Google search

Public domain illustrations.

Paintings; Michael Earney

Reviews: If you enjoyed this book, Michael P. Earney would appreciate it if you would leave a review on Amazon, Goodreads, or any other Review site you like.

Also, don't forget to tell your friends! Word of mouth advertising is the most precious ***"Thank You"*** a reader can ever give an author.

About the Author: Michael P. Earney is a fine arts painter who grew up in England. His writer's voice reflects curiosity and passion for the world of nature. His text is instructive yet playful. The illustrations are executed with grace and fine detail. Earney is in his element as artist, writer, educator, and naturalist. To learn more about this author's books and various achievements please visit his websites.

Contact Mr. Earney: themichaelearney@yahoo.com

Websites: www.MichaelEarney.com and www.EarneyWorks.com

Publisher: http://www.ErinGoBraghPublishing.com/authors/mearney

Texas Authors:

http://authors.txauthors.com/index.php/authors-listing-by-first-name-l-p/authors-m/michael-earney

www.ingramcontent.com/pod-product-compliance
Lightning Source LLC
Chambersburg PA
CBHW042320210526
45473CB00007B/2401